2014-2015

Middle School
Test Materials

ISBN-978-1-329-53259-5

2014-2015 Middle School Test Materials

Table of Contents

Thank you for purchasing the 2014-2015 mathleague.org test series. Good luck to you and your students as you prepare for this year's math contests! Upcoming tournament information and the latest mathleague.org policies and information can be found at our website, http://mathleague.org, and you can reach us at mathleague@mathleague.org or 415-662-8454.

mathleague.org is eager to help bring local math contests and championship meets to areas where such opportunities do not currently exist. Feel free to contact us if you would like more information on hosting a local contest or setting up a mathleague.org championship in your state or province.

Please be sure to let us know if you find typographical or mathematical errors. All tests are copyright 2014 and/or 2015 by mathleague.org and may be photocopied for practice within your school but may not be distributed outside your school.

This page intentionally left blank.
[sic]

Sprint Test
Round 11511

Name: _____

Grade: _____

School: _____

place ID sticker inside this box

Score: #1 _____ Scorer's Initials _____

Score: #2 _____ Scorer's Initials _____

1. 16	2. 96 hours	3. 65	4.	5.
6.	7. 9	8. 5760	9.	10. 9
11.	12.	13. 2/6	14.	15.
16.	17.	18.	19. 51	20. 3
21.	22.	23.	24.	25.
26. 31	27.	28.	29.	30.

1. Let $a \oslash b = \frac{a \cdot b}{2}$. If $x \oslash 24 = 192$, compute x.

2. Steve works 8 hours on every weekday, and 4 hours on every weekend day. How many hours does Steve work during 2 weeks, each from Monday through Sunday?

3. What is the sum of all integers between -10 and 15, inclusive?

4. Together, Sherry and Joe can paint a house in 6 hours. If Sherry and Joe also work with Painter Jill, the three of them can paint the house in 2 hours. How many hours does it take Painter Jill to paint a house on her own?

5. An equilateral triangle with area $64\sqrt{3}$ has the same perimeter as a square. What is the area of the square?

6. Three participants are in a race. Bob, one of the participants, is slow and will not come in first place. In how many orderings can the three racers cross the finish line, assuming there are no ties?

7. How many positive divisors does 36 have?

8. Compute $\frac{7! + 6!}{8}$.

9. Each Fibonacci number is the sum of the previous two. The first Fibonacci number is 1, the second is 2, the thirteenth is 233, and the fifteenth is 610. Find the fourteenth Fibonacci number.

10. Compute the sum of the digits of $123456789 + 987654321$.

11. Find the maximum element of $\{\frac{1}{2-3}, \frac{1}{2^3}, \frac{1}{2 \cdot 3}, \frac{1}{2+3}, \frac{1}{23}\}$.

12. Joe has exactly 10 minutes to use a toaster, which can hold 3 slices of bread at a time. Joe has 5 slices of bread, and wishes to give each slice an equal amount of time in the toaster. Assuming he removes and inserts slices of bread into the toaster instantaneously, and each slice spends the same amount of time in the toaster, what is the maximum number of minutes for which he can toast each slice?

13. Joe rolls a die three times. What is the probability that at least one of his rolls is a multiple of 3? Express your answer as a common fraction.

14. Let k be the value such that the lines $y = 3x + 2$, $y = 4$, and $y = kx + 6$ have exactly one intersection point. Compute k^2.

15. For positive real numbers a, b, c, we have $ab = 8$, $bc = 6$, and $ca = 12$. Compute the sum of the squares of a, b and c.

16. What is the largest prime number that divides the quantity $(19! - 17!)$?

17. Compute the area enclosed by the region $|\frac{x}{2}| + |\frac{y}{2}| = 3$.

18. An equilateral triangle with side length 6 is inscribed in a circle. If the radius of the circle can be expressed in simplest radical form as $p\sqrt{q}$, compute $p + q$.

19. Compute the smallest integer greater than 50 with exactly five positive divisors.

20. What is the largest positive integer n such that $2^8 \cdot 4^4 \cdot 8^2 \cdot 16^1$ is divisible by 2^n?

21. An ant is crawling on a number line, starting at 0. Every minute starting at the end of the 1st minute, it moves 1 unit in either the positive direction or the negative direction with equal probability. After 9 minutes, let P be the probability that the ant is within 1 unit of the point -3. Compute P and express your answer as a common fraction.

22. Jimmy draws a regular hexagon $ABCDEF$ and regular pentagon $ABGHI$ in the same plane, such that G, H, and I are *not* in the interior of $ABCDEF$. What is the number of degrees in angle CBG?

23. Evan drinks lemonade before his math contests, which he makes by mixing lemon juice and sugar water. Before taking the mathleague.org contest, he needs an extra boost, so he doubles the volume of lemon juice in his drink without changing the volume of sugar water. Evan's lemonade is now 8% lemon juice (by volume). What is the ratio of lemon juice to sugar water in Evan's normal drink? Express your answer as a common fraction.

24. Compute the product of all possible values of x that satisfy the equation $27^{x^2+3x+4} = 3^{5x-9}$.

25. All of the side lengths in a right rectangular prism are positive integers. If the space diagonal connecting the two opposite vertices of the rectangular prism has length 7, what is the volume of the prism?

26. In an elimination tennis tournament with 32 entrants, a player is eliminated when they lose a single match, and the champion is the last player remaining. In total, how many matches are played to determine the champion?

27. In a regular octahedron with side length 8, let the length of the segment connecting the two vertices furthest from each other be ℓ. If $\ell = a\sqrt{b}$ in simplest radical form, compute a^b.

28. Let x be a positive integer such that $x^5 = 503,284,375$. Find x.

29. A number is called *normal* if it has the property that its digits are not in strictly increasing or strictly decreasing order. How many 3-digit numbers are normal? (e.g. 566 is normal, but 567 is not.)

30. Three congruent circles with radius 6 are drawn such that each pair of circles is externally tangent. A smaller circle with radius r is drawn such that it is externally tangent

to all three of the circles. If r can be expressed in simplest radical form as $a\sqrt{b} - c$ where a, b, c are integers, compute $a \cdot c - b$.

mathleague.org

Target Test
Round 11511

1. Seashells by the seashore can be bought singly for 12 cents each, or in sets of 8 for $1. What is the greatest number of seashells that Sally can buy with $3.25?

1.

2. Glinda and Ozma are shopping at Dorothy's Doodads. Glinda buys four slinkys and five kittens for $53. Ozma buys two slinkys and two kittens for $22. How much does a kitten cost at Dorothy's Doodads?

2.

Name: _____

Grade: _____

School: _____

place ID sticker inside this box

Score: #3 _____ Scorer's Initials _____

Score: #4 _____ Scorer's Initials _____

3. Compute the hundreds digit of $2014 \cdot 2013 \cdot 2012 \cdot 2011$.

3.

4. If *equiangular* hexagon $ABCDEF$ has $AB = 3, BC = 2, CD = 6$, and $DE = 4$, what is its perimeter?

4.

Name: _____

Grade: _____

School: _____

place ID sticker inside this box

Score: #5 _____ Scorer's Initials _____

Score: #6 _____ Scorer's Initials _____

5. Let N be the largest multiple of 3 with all distinct digits. Find the ones digit of N.

5.

6. Let $n = \sqrt{2}$. Compute the remainder when n^{2014} is divided by 1000.

6.

Name: _____

Grade: _____

School: _____

place ID sticker inside this box

Score: #7 _____ Scorer's Initials _____

Score: #8 _____ Scorer's Initials _____

7. A triangle of height s is constructed on each side of a square of side length s, using the side of the square as the base. The total area of the new figure (triangles and square) is 12. Compute s.

7.

8. Let R and S be two nonzero geometric sequences with equal common ratios. The first term of R is half the first term of S. If the sum of the first 12 terms of R divided by the sum of the first 6 terms of S is equal to 365, compute the common ratio of the two sequences.

8.

Team Test
Round 11511

School/
Team:

Score: #1 _____ Scorer's Initials _____

Score: #2 _____ Scorer's Initials _____

name or ID sticker goes in this box	name or ID sticker goes in this box
name or ID sticker goes in this box	name or ID sticker goes in this box
name or ID sticker goes in this box	name or ID sticker goes in this box

1.

2.

3.

4.

5.

6.

7.

8.

9.

10.

1. Bob constructs a square from 16 smaller square that are all the same size. How many squares of any size are there in the bigger square (including itself)?

2. Ladislaus runs a very popular bakery. To try to keep up with the demand, each day he bakes as many cakes as he did in the previous two days together. If he bakes two cakes on Monday and five cakes on Tuesday, how many will he bake that Sunday?

3. Circe has n identical cubical blocks and uses them to build a rectangular prism of height 10. Then Odysseus arrives with $7n$ more blocks, all identical to the original n. Circe knocks down her prism and builds a new prism out of all the blocks, in the same proportions as the old one. Compute the height of the new prism.

4. Circle O and quadrilateral $ABCD$ intersect in n points, but their interiors are disjoint (i.e. they have no area in common). Find the greatest possible value of n.

5. The reflection of the point (1, 3) across (a, b) is (13, 7). Find (a, b).

6. A diemaker can carve any digit into a die in four minutes. It takes him one hour to carve the integers from 1 to n in base 10 into the sides of a certain die. Find n.

7. A cuboctahedron is a convex polyhedron with 14 faces and 24 edges. All of its faces are either squares or triangles. Compute how many are squares.

8. Define S to be the set of factors of 300 which are not divisible by any perfect square greater than 1. Compute the number of elements of S.

9. Three friends have five different candy bars to eat. How many ways are there to choose who eats which candy bars, if they don't necessarily have to eat all the candy bars?

10. How many 3-digit numbers ABC (where A, B, and C are base-10 digits) can be formed if $A + B + C = 12$?

1. What is the sum of all the angles on all of the faces of a square pyramid, in degrees?

2. Round 1.1^5 to the nearest tenth.

3. Convert $\frac{\pi}{3}$ radians to degrees.

4. Two quarters and a dime are flipped. What is the probability that the total value of the coins showing heads is greater than 30 cents? Express your answer as a common fraction.

5. Bob the builder wants to build a cube, but he needs to purchase faces, edges, and vertices for the cube at a local hardware store. Faces costs $4 each, edges cost $2 each, and vertices cost $3 each. How many dollars does Bob need to purchase enough materials to build a cube?

6. A square is inscribed in another square with an area of 256 m^2 (each vertex of the smaller square lies on an edge of the larger square). What is the least possible area of the inscribed square, in square meters?

7. What is the ninth number in the ninth row of Pascal's triangle? (Remember the top row is the 0th row, and each row starts with the 0th entry).

8. Simplify: $(4n)^5 \cdot (5n)^4$.

9. What is the smallest possible area of a right triangle such that its shortest side has a length of 6?

10. Valerie took a math class that started at 11:50 AM and ended at 1:24 PM that same day. How many minutes did the math class last?

11. Compute the sum of the positive divisors of 2014.

12. What is the average value of all of the numbers in the seventh row of Pascal's triangle? (Remember the top row is the 0th row).

13. If one angle in an isosceles triangle has a measure of $42°$, what is the smallest possible measure of the largest angle in the triangle, in degrees?

14. What is the longest possible hypotenuse of a $30° - 60° - 90°$ triangle such that one of its sides has a length of 5 cm?

15. What is the smallest natural number with exactly 5 positive divisors?

16. The formula to convert from Celsius to Fahrenheit is $F = \frac{9}{5}C + 32$. What value of F is twice the corresponding value of C?

17. How many positive divisors does 785 have?

18. What is the volume of a cylinder with radius 3 and height 5?

19. If 12 more than a number is equal to 24 less than the absolute value of the number, what is the number?

20. Compute: $\frac{1}{1\cdot2} + \frac{1}{2\cdot3} + \frac{1}{3\cdot4} + \frac{1}{4\cdot5}$. Express your answer as a common fraction.

21. What is the distance between the points (23, 18) and (14, 30)?

22. x is 25% larger than y, y is 60% larger than z, and x is N% larger than z. Compute N.

23. Compute the product of the reciprocals of the first five positive integers. Express your answer as a common fraction.

24. How many positive divisors does $2^5 \cdot 3^4 \cdot 4^3 \cdot 5^2$ have?

25. Luis only got red, blue, and green peppermints when he went trick-or-treating during Halloween. He received 19 peppermints total, of which 4 were blue. If the number of green peppermints he received is a multiple of 7, what is the least number of red peppermints he could've received?

26. Compute: $1 \cdot 1! + 2 \cdot 2! + 3 \cdot 3! + 4 \cdot 4!$

27. If the first and second terms of a sequence are 3 and 1, respectively, and every term after the second is the sum of the previous two terms, what is the eighth term in the sequence?

28. A triangle has two of its vertices on a circle and its third vertex at the center of the same circle. If the radius of the circle is 24 cm, what is the maximum possible area of the triangle, in square centimeters?

29. David went to a toy shop to buy some miniature cars. If there are a total of 8 different cars he can choose from, how many ways can he choose 2 cars to purchase?

30. Compute the sum of the infinite geometric series $\frac{2}{3} + \frac{4}{9} + \frac{8}{27} + \frac{16}{81} + \cdots$

31. During the summer, Katherine saved 300 dollars in June, 500 dollars in July, and 450 dollars in August. How many dollars did she save over the summer?

32. Kenneth drove at 60 mph for 6 hours and 40 mph for 4 hours during his trip. What was his average speed during the trip, in mph?

33. If three sides of a trapezoid have a length of 5 cm and the last side has a length of 11 cm, what is the area of the trapezoid, in square centimeters?

34. What is the least common multiple of 1, 2, 3, 4, 5, and 6?

35. If segment AB is the diameter of a circle with a circumference of 22π cm, what is the distance from the midpoint of AB to A, in cm?

36. How many degrees are in each interior angle of a regular nonagon?

37. If a line goes through the points $(3, 6)$, $(12, 0)$, and $(a, a - 2)$, what is the value of a?

38. What is the length, in cm, of the interior diagonal of a rectangular prism such that 3 of its edges have a length of 12 cm, 16 cm, and 21 cm?

39. If $2a + b + c = 19$, $a + 2b + c = 34$, and $a + b + 2c = 15$, find the value of $a + b + c$.

40. Stephen needs 31 pencils. If pencils are sold in packs of 7, what is the least number of packs of pencils Stephen needs to purchase?

41. A fundraiser sold 1000 raffle tickets at $4 each. One ticket won $500 and five tickets each won $100. If Joan bought a ticket, what is the expected number of dollars she would win?

42. $f(x)$ is a function of the form $ax + b$. If $f(1) = 5$ and $f(7) = 9.2$, compute the value of $a + b$.

43. A car drives 350 miles at 56 mph. How many minutes did the car drive?

44. The number $(2 + \sqrt{3})(2 - \sqrt{2})^2$ can be rewritten in the form $a + b\sqrt{2} + c\sqrt{3} + d\sqrt{6}$, where a, b, c, and d are integers. What is the value of $a + b + c + d$?

45. Compute the sum of all prime numbers less than 100 that contain the digit 7 at least once.

46. From point A, Martin walked 12 meters north, 5 meters east, 4 meters south, and 10 meters east, to point B. What is the length of AB, in meters?

47. If a and b are integers such that $a^b - 1 = 80$, what is the least possible value of a?

48. How many prime numbers are divisible by 133?

49. A book is opened exactly in the middle. Assuming the book's pages are numbered properly, and the sum of the two visible page numbers is 1337, how many pages are in the book?

50. In triangle ABC, the measure of angle A is $2x$ degrees, the measure of angle B is $3x$ degrees, and the measure of angle C is $4x$ degrees. What is x?

51. What is the product of the two largest primes less than 100?

52. Compute the value of $2013^2 - (2011)(2015)$.

53. What is the remainder when 7^{1470} is divided by 100?

54. Philip counted 36 tires in a parking lot with only cars and motorcycles. If there were more motorcycles than cars, what is the largest possible number of cars in the parking lot? Remember cars have 4 tires and motorcycles have 2.

55. If $4(3 - 6x) + 2x - 1 = ax + b$, compute the ordered pair (a, b).

56. How many diagonals does a regular decagon have?

57. Compute: $9^3 + 3 \cdot 9^2 + 3 \cdot 9 + 1$.

58. What is the area of an equilateral triangle inscribed in a circle with a radius of 2? Express your answer in simplest radical form.

59. How many integers less than 100,000 have the product of their digits equal to 117?

60. What is the greatest possible value of $a \cdot b \cdot c$, where a, b, and c are distinct elements of the set $\{-5, -7, 2, -3, 1\}$?

61. 10 people try out for a dodgeball team. How many ways are there to pick a 5-person starting lineup from these 10?

62. A 2x2x2 cube, made up of 8 unit cubes, is painted on all of the faces exterior to the 2x2x2 cube. What percent of the total surface area of the unit cubes is painted?

63. Roberta was bored, so she decided to write the first 456 positive integers and count the number of digits she wrote. Assuming she didn't make any mistakes, what number did she get when she counted the digits she wrote?

64. Compute: $1^2 + 2^2 + 3^2 + 4^2 + 5^2 + 6^2$.

65. A straight 60-foot long fence has 6 posts evenly spaced along the fence, including a post at each end. What is the distance between two consecutive posts, in feet?

66. If $f(x) = \sqrt{2x} + 3$, compute $f(2) + f(8)$.

67. Express 333 in base 3.

68. What is the largest possible number of primes between two consecutive multiples of 10?

69. If a random card is chosen from a standard 52-card deck (13 different ranks in each of four suits), what is the probability that it has a number (between 2 and 10, inclusive) for its rank? Express your answer as a common fraction.

70. How many integers between 1000 and 2000, inclusive, contain at most 3 even digits?

71. 90 people filled up $\frac{2}{5}$ of the seats in an auditorium. How many seats does the auditorium have?

72. If $\log 2014$ can be expressed as $\log a + \log b$ where a and b are integers, what is ab?

73. What is $\frac{1}{3}\%$ of 6000?

74. If three numbers are in the ratio 3:4:5 and their sum is -84, what is the greatest of the numbers?

75. If three standard six-sided dice are rolled, what is the probability that the sum of the numbers on the dice equals 5? Express your answer as a common fraction.

76. The geometric mean of 9 and x is 12. What is the value of x?

77. What is the sum of the digits in the decimal expansion of $2^4 \cdot 3^4 \cdot 5^4$?

78. Compute the sum of the distinct prime factors of 8888.

79. What is the greatest common factor of 2014 and 570?

80. The equation $x^2 + 4x + 5 = 8$ has two solutions, a and b. What is the value of $4(a + b) + 5ab$?

Sprint Test

1. 16
2. 96
3. 65
4. 3
5. 144
6. 4
7. 9
8. 720
9. 377
10. 9
11. $\frac{1}{2+3}$
12. 6
13. $\frac{19}{27}$
14. 9
15. 29
16. 31
17. 72
18. 5
19. 81
20. 26
21. $\frac{21}{128}$
22. 132
23. $\frac{1}{23}$
24. 7
25. 36

26. 31
27. 64
28. 55
29. 696
30. 21

Target Test

1. 27
2. ($) 9
3. 0
4. 23
5. 0
6. 128
7. 2
8. 3

Team Test

1. 30
2. 50
3. 20
4. 2
5. (7,5)
6. 12
7. 6
8. 8
9. 1024
10. 66

Countdown

1. 1080(°)
2. 1.6
3. 60(°)
4. $\frac{1}{2}$
5. ($)72
6. 128 (m²)
7. 1
8. $640,000n^9$
9. 18
10. 94 (minutes)
11. 3240
12. 16
13. 69(°)
14. 10 (cm)
15. 16
16. 320
17. 4
18. 45π
19. -18
20. $\frac{4}{5}$
21. 15
22. 100(%)
23. $\frac{1}{120}$
24. 180
25. 1
26. 119

27. 37
28. 288 (cm²)
29. 28
30. 2
31. ($)1250
32. 52 (mph)
33. 32 (cm²)
34. 60
35. 11 (cm)
36. 140(°)
37. 6
38. 29 (cm)
39. 17
40. 5 (packs)
41. ($)1
42. 5
43. 375 (minutes)
44. 6
45. 495
46. 17 (m)
47. -9
48. 0
49. 1336 (pages)
50. 20
51. 8633
52. 4
53. 49

54. 5 (cars)
55. $(-22, 11)$
56. 35 (diagonals)
57. 1000
58. $3\sqrt{3}$
59. 0 (integers)
60. 70
61. 252
62. 50%
63. 1260
64. 91
65. 12 (feet)
66. 12
67. 110100_3
68. 4 (primes)
69. $\frac{9}{13}$
70. 1000 (integers)
71. 225 (seats)
72. 2014
73. 20
74. -21
75. $\frac{1}{36}$
76. 16
77. 9
78. 114
79. 38
80. -31

Sprint Test Solutions

1. We have $24x/2 = 192$, so $x = 16$.

2. Tim works $8 \cdot 5 + 2 \cdot 4 = 48$ hours per week, so he works 96 hours in two weeks.

3. The other terms cancel out, and we are left with $11 + 12 + 13 + 14 + 15 = 65$.

4. Let Painter Jill paint $\frac{1}{x}$ houses per hour. Then, since Sherry and Joe working with Painter Jill can paint the house in 2 hours, we have $\frac{2}{6} + \frac{2}{x} = 1$, so $x = 3$.

5. Let a side of the triangle be $2x$. Then half of a side is x, and the altitude is then $x\sqrt{3}$. So the area of the triangle is $x^2\sqrt{3}$. So $x = 8$ and the perimeter is 48. Then a side length of a square with the same perimeter is 12 and so the area of the square is 144.

6. There are 2 ways to choose Bob's place, either 2nd or 3rd. Then either of the other competitors could be 1st for 2 more choices in each case, for a total of 4.

7. $36 = 2^2 \cdot 3^2$, so it has $(2+1)^2 = 9$ divisors. That's how the cool kids do it. The others will just accurately count without missing anything.

8. $7! = 7 \cdot 6 \cdot 5 \cdots 2 \cdot 1 = 7 \cdot 6!$, so $7! + 6! = 7 \cdot 6! + 6! = 8 \cdot 6!$. So $\frac{7!+6!}{8} = \frac{8 \cdot 6!}{8} = 6! = 6 \cdot 5 \cdot 4 \cdot 3 \cdot 2 \cdot 1 = 720$.

9. By the definition of the Fibonacci numbers, the thirteenth number plus the fourteenth number equals the fifteenth number. So the fourteenth number must equal the fifteenth number minus the thirteenth number, or $610 - 233 = 377$.

10. Each pair of digits sums to 10, so the ones digit is zero and the next nine digits are each a carried 1.

11. All the fractions have numerator 1, so the largest one will be the one with the smallest (positive) denominator. The denominators are $2 - 3 = -1$, $2^3 = 8$, $2 \cdot 3 = 6$, $2 + 3 = 5$, and 23 respectively. The smallest positive value among these is 5, so the maximal fraction is $\frac{1}{2+3}$.

12. He has $10 \cdot 3 = 30$ effective minutes of toasting time. Since there are 5 slices, each slice gets $30/5 = 6$ minutes of toasting time.

13. The probability that his roll is not a multiple of three on any given roll is $\frac{2}{3}$. The probability that he does not get a multiple of 3 on three given rolls is thus $\left(\frac{2}{3}\right)^3 = \frac{8}{27}$, so the probability that he gets at least one multiple of three is then $1 - \frac{8}{27} = \frac{19}{27}$.

14. The lines $y = 3x + 2$ and $y = 4$ intersect at $\left(\frac{2}{3}, 4\right)$. Plugging this point into the third equation, we have $4 = \frac{2k}{3} + 6$ and then $-6 = 2k$, so $k^2 = 9$.

15. Multiplying all three equations gives $a^2 b^2 c^2 = 576$. Then $a^2 = \frac{576}{(bc)^2} = 16$, and similarly $b^2 = 4$ and $c^2 = 9$. So $a^2 + b^2 + c^2 = 29$.

16. Factor the expression as $17!(19 \cdot 18 - 1) = 17!(341) = 17! \cdot 31 \cdot 11$, so the answer is 31.

17. Since the factor of $\frac{1}{2}$ can be taken out of the absolute values on the LHS, our problem is equivalent to finding the area enclosed by the graph of $|x| + |y| = 6$. Note that this area is a square with vertices $(6, 0), (0, 6), (-6, 0), (0, -6)$, so the area is $(6\sqrt{2})^2 = 72$.

18. Let the triangle be $\triangle ABC$, call the center of the circle O, and call the foot of the altitude from A point H. We have $BH = 3$, $AH = 3\sqrt{3}$. Since OHB is a $30 - 60 - 90$ right triangle, $OH = \sqrt{3}$ and $OB = 2\sqrt{3}$, so our answer is $2 + 3 = 5$.

19. To have 5 factors, a number must have the form of p^4, with p prime. The first p that works is 3. You should look up how to find the number of factors of a number if you don't understand this.

20. This product is equal to $2^8 \cdot (2^2)^4 \cdot (2^3)^2 \cdot 2^4 = 2^8 \cdot 2^8 \cdot 2^6 \cdot 2^4 = 2^{26}$, so the largest power of 2 dividing it is itself.

21. The ant can either end at $-4, -3$, or -2. However, after an odd number of moves, it can only end at an odd number. Thus, we just have to

compute the probability that the ant ends at -3. It must have moved to the left 6 times and to the right 3 times. The number of ways to move to the right exactly 3 times in 9 chances is $\binom{9}{3} = 84$, and the probability of each of these 84 sequences occurring is $\frac{1}{2^9}$. The total probability of ending at -3 is then $\frac{84}{2^9} = \frac{21}{128}$.

22. $\angle ABC$ has a measure of 120 degrees, and $\angle ABG$ has a measure of 108 degrees. Therefore $\angle CBG = 360 - 120 - 108 = 132$ degrees.

23. Suppose Evan makes 100 ounces of strong lemonade. Then this drink consists of 8oz of lemon juice and 92 oz of sugar water. Normally, he uses 4oz of lemon juice and 92oz of sugar water, for a total of 96oz of lemonade. This is a ratio of $\frac{4}{92} = \frac{1}{23}$.

24. We can write the equation as $3^{3x^2+9x+12} = 3^{5x-9}$ which gives $3x^2 + 9x + 12 = 5x - 9$. This simplifies to $3x^2 + 4x + 21 = 0$, or $x^2 + \frac{4}{3}x + 7 = 0$. If this factors as $(x - r)(x - s)$, then we have $rs = 7$.

25. If we let the width, height, and length be a, b, c respectively, we have $(\sqrt{a^2 + b^2})^2 + c^2 = 49$, which simplifies to $a^2 + b^2 + c^2 = 49$. A bit of experimentation with integer values for a, b, c shows that the only solution is $a = 6$, $b = 3$, $c = 2$, so the volume is 36.

26. It takes each player one match to be eliminated, so it will take 31 matches to determine a champion.

Target Test Solutions

1. $\frac{100}{8} = 12.5$, so it's actually more expensive to buy seashells in sets of 8 than singly. So Sally should buy her seashells singly in order to get as many as possible. $12 \cdot 27 = 324$, so Sally can buy 27 seashells (and will have 1 cent left over).

2. If two slinkys and two kittens cost \$22, then four slinkys and four kittens cost \$44. Glinda paid \$53 four four slinkys and five kittens, so

27. Let P and Q be two opposite vertices of the octahedron. Then there are two other vertices, X and Y, such that $PXQY$ is a square, and all of its sides are edges of the octahedron. Since PQ is a diagonal of this square, $PQ = 8\sqrt{2}$, and the answer is 64.

28. Note that the only way x^5 can end is 5 is for x itself to end in 5. Now we can use a simple bounding argument by noticing that $50^5 = 312,500,000$ and $60^5 = 777,600,000$ and x^5 is between these two numbers, so $50 < x < 60$ and therefore $x = 55$.

29. There are $\binom{9}{3} = 84$ 3-digit numbers with digits in strictly increasing order, since given any choice of 3 distinct nonzero digits, there is exactly one way to put them in increasing order. Similarly, there are $\binom{10}{3} = 120$ with digits in strictly decreasing order, since we can use 0 as a digit now. There are 900 3-digit numbers, so our answer is $900 - 84 - 120 = 696$.

30. Let A, B, and C be the centers of the three congruent circles. These from an equilateral triangle with side length 12. Let O be the center of the smaller circle. By symmetry, O is the center of triangle ABC. Let H be the foot of the altitude from A to BC. Since ABH is a 30-60-90 right triangle, $AH = 6\sqrt{3}$. Also, $AO = 6 + r$, so $OH = 6\sqrt{3} - 6 - r$. Also, BHO is a 30-60-90 right triangle, and $BO = 2OH$. But $BO = AO = 6 + r$, from which $6 + r = 12\sqrt{3} - 12 - 2r$, and $6 + r = 4\sqrt{3}$. Thus $r = 4\sqrt{3} - 6$, and the answer is $4 \cdot 6 - 3 = 21$.

the extra kitten must have cost the extra \$53 - \$44 = \$9.

3. Only the last 3 digits matter, so we find the hundreds digit of $14 \cdot 13 \cdot 12 \cdot 11$.

4. An equiangular hexagon can be turned into an equilateral triangle by "gluing" equilateral triangles to every other side. In this hexagon, if we glue triangles to BC, DE, and AF, the side length of the resulting equilateral triangle

is equal to $BC + CD + DE = 12$. Thus $AF = 12 - AB - BC = 7$, and $EF = 12 - AF - DE = 1$, so the perimeter is $3 + 2 + 6 + 4 + 1 + 7 = 23$.

5. The largest multiple of three with all distinct digits will certainly have a zero as one of its digits; otherwise the same number multiplied by 10 (thus ending in a zero) would be a larger multiple of three that still had all distinct digits. A number is a multiple of 3 exactly when the sum of its digits is a multiple of 3, so once the digits are chosen their ordering is irrelevant to the divisibility criterion. Therefore, the digits of the number will be ordered from largest to smallest in order to maximize its size; so zero will always be the ones digit.

6. We want to find $2^{1007} \mod 1000$. We can split this up into finding $2^{1007} \mod 8$ and $2^{1007} \mod 125$. The former is just 0. Now we work modulo 125. Since $2^7 \equiv 3$, we have $2^{1001} \equiv (2^7)^{143} = 3^{143}$. Then $3^5 \equiv -7$, so $3^{140} \equiv (-7)^{28} \equiv 7^{28}$. Then $7^4 = 2401 \equiv 26$, so $7^{28} \equiv 26^7$. Also,

$26^2 \equiv 51$, so $26^7 \equiv 51^3 \cdot 26 \equiv 151 \cdot 26 \equiv 26^2 \equiv 51$. Working backwards, then, we have $7^{28} \equiv 26^7 \equiv 51$, and $3^{143} \equiv 27 \cdot 3^{140} \equiv 27 \cdot 51 \equiv 2$, and $2^{1007} \equiv 64 \cdot 2 \equiv 128 \equiv 3$. The unique solution (mod 1000) of $k \equiv 0 \mod 8$ and $k \equiv 3 \mod 125$ is $k = 128$, so that is our answer.

7. The area of a square of side length s is s^2, while the area of a triangle with base and height both s is $\frac{s^2}{2}$. So four triangles plus one square have an area of $4\frac{s^2}{2} + s^2 = 3s^2$ altogether. Therefore $3s^2 = 12$, so $s^2 = 4$ and $s = \pm 2$. A square cannot have a negative side length, so s must be 2.

8. Let the first term of R be a. Then the second term of S is $2a$. The sum of the first 12 terms of R is $\frac{a(1-r^{12})}{1-r}$, and the sum of the first 6 terms of S is $\frac{2a(1-r^6)}{1-r}$. Dividing the two sums and cancelling gives $\frac{1-r^{12}}{2(1-r^6)} = 365$. The left side is equal to $\frac{1}{2}(1 + r^6)$, so $r^6 = 2 \cdot 365 - 1 = 729$, and thus $r = 3$.

Team Test Solutions

1. There are of course 16 of the smaller squares. There are 9 squares with twice the small square's side lenght, 4 with three times the length, and also the 1 big square.

2. The number of cakes Ladislaus bakes each day forms a sequence $\{a_n\}$ where $a_1 = 2$, $a_2 = 5$, and $a_n = a_{n-1} + a_{n-2}$. The question asks for a_7. Fortunately the first several terms are easily calculated by addition: $2 + 5 = 7$, $5 + 7 = 12$, $7 + 12 = 19$, $12 + 19 = 31$, $31 + 19 = 50 = a_7$.

3. After Odysseus arrives, Circe has $n + 7n = 8n$ blocks to work with. She can therefore double her prism in each dimension, which since it is three-dimensional will multiply the volume by $2 \cdot 2 \cdot 2 = 8$, using all the blocks while retaining the proportions. So the new height is twice the old height of 10, or 20.

4. A circle can only touch a convex quadrilateral

at one point, if their interiors do not intersect. However, if the quadrilateral is concave (which the problem statement permits) it may make a v-shape and thus touch the circle at two points. The two interiors do not intersect, so each side of the quadrilateral can touch the circle at one point at most. Moreover, if three sides touch the circle, then adding the fourth side will cause the quadrilateral and circle to have area in common. Therefore two points of tangency is the maximum that can be achieved.

5. Reflecting (1, 3) across (a, b) will extend the line between the two points an equal distance in the opposite direction, reaching (13, 7). So (a, b) will lie exactly halfway between (1, 3) and (13, 7); so (a, b) = $(\frac{1+13}{2}, \frac{3+7}{2})$ = (7, 5).

6. One hour is 60 minutes, so the diemaker must have carved $\frac{60}{4} = 15$ digits into the die. The numbers from 1 to 9 use nine digits, leaving six. Numbers greater than 9 and less than 100 have two digits each, so six digits can make up

three more numbers: 10, 11, and 12.

7. Each edge borders 2 faces, so the 14 faces must have $24 \cdot 2 = 48$ edges in total. Let s be the number of square faces and $14 - s$ the number of triangular faces; then $4s + 3(14 - s) = 48$. Simplifying, $s + 42 = 48$ so $s = 6$.

8. First, find the prime factorization: $300 = 2^2 \cdot 3 \cdot 5^2$. Any element s of S must be composed of these factors. No prime factor p can appear more than once in s, or s will be divisible by p^2, a perfect square. So to construct an element of S, we choose whether to include each of 2, 3 and 5 in the product, for $2 \cdot 2 \cdot 2 = 8$ possibilities, which is therefore the number of elements of S.

9. For each candy bar, the friends have four choices: give it to the first friend, give it to the second friend, give it to the third friend, or don't eat it. So there are $4^5 = 1024$ total choices for the distribution of the candy bars.

10. Without restrictions on A, B, C, we want to find the number of solutions to $A + B + C = 12$. By Stars and Bars, there are $\binom{14}{2} = 91$ ways to choose such triples (A, B, C). However, we must subtract from this total the numbers that have digits larger than 9, or that have $A = 0$. For digits larger than 9, the first case is $12 - 0 - 0$, which can occur in 3 ways. The next case is $11 - 1 - 0$ which can happen in 6 ways. Then there are the cases $10 - 1 - 1$ and $10 - 2 - 0$ which can occur in 3 and 6 ways respectively. Finally we must subtract off the cases that we have not accounted for where $A = 0$, of which there are 7, specifically $(0, 3, 9), (0, 4, 8), \cdots, (0, 9, 3)$. After accounting for digit restrictions, there are $91 - 18 - 7 = 66$ possible triples (A, B, C).

Sprint Test
Round 11512

Name: _____

Grade: _____

School: _____

place ID sticker inside this box

Score: #1 _____ Scorer's Initials _____

Score: #2 _____ Scorer's Initials _____

1.	2.	3.	4.	5.
6.	7.	8.	9.	10.
11.	12.	13.	14.	15.
16.	17.	18.	19.	20.
21.	22.	23.	24.	25.
26.	27.	28.	29.	30.

1. What is the largest square number less than 1000?

2. Solve for x if $3x + 14 = -7x - 68$. Express your answer as a decimal.

3. Find the area of a circle with circumference 32π. Express your answer in terms of π.

4. Compute 2014^3.

5. Compute $(1 + 2 \cdot 3^4) - (4 - 5 \cdot (6 + 7))$.

6. There are 12 candidates in a city election. The winner will be the mayor, and the runner-up will be the vice-mayor. How many different combinations of mayor and vice-mayor are possible?

7. Find the volume of a cube with side length 12.

8. What is the product of the prime factors of 2014?

9. How many two-digit numbers have a units digit larger than the tens digit?

10. How many two-digit numbers have a tens digit larger than the units digit?

11. Find the area of a circle with circumference 32. Express your answer in terms of π.

12. A sphere of radius 2 is centered at O. Circle $\mathfrak{C}$ lies entirely on the surface of the sphere, and the radius of $\mathfrak{C}$ is $\frac{\sqrt{5}}{2}$. If P lies on $\mathfrak{C}$, find OP.

13. Find the sum of all values of x for which $\sqrt{2 + x} = x$.

14. Utnapishtim (a stuffed raccoon), abetted by his human friend Kaylene, wrecks Kaylene's family's new and still-uninsured minivan. Kaylene's parents rule that the rascally racoon must pay off the entire loan himself. The principal (original amount of money borrowed) is $20,000. The loan has a rate of 6.5% annual simple interest. The term (length of time) of the loan is 5 years. He is responsible for all the principal plus all the interest. How many total dollars does Utnapisthim owe his adoptive parents?

15. Refer to the problem above. Kaylene, in a surprising display of guilty conscience, offers to to pay for half the total cost of the loan out of her college fund. Utnapishtim must pay the other half. Assuming he pays his entire allowance of $10 per month towards the loan, how many years will it take to repay? Express your answer as a decimal rounded to the nearest tenth.

16. Rachel and Michael are trying to find each other, but they are terrible at communicating locations to each other. Rachel starts out being exactly eighty meters due west of Michael. She walks fifty meters north, turns and walks a hundred meters west, then turns again and walks thirty meters south. Michael walks fifty meters south, then

turns and walks sixty meters east. In meters, how far apart from each other are they now?

17. In triangle ABC, $AB = 13$, $BC = 14$, $CA = 15$. If H is the foot of the altitude from A to side BC and M is the midpoint of side BC, what is the length of MH?

18. If p, q, and r are the solutions to the equation $x^3 + 2x^2 + 3x + 4 = 0$, what is $p^2qr + pq^2r + pqr^2$? If appropriate, express your answer as a common fraction.

19. If p, q, and r are the solutions to the equation $x^3 + 2x^2 + 3x + 4 = 0$, what is $\frac{1}{p} + \frac{1}{q} + \frac{1}{r}$? If appropriate, express your answer as a common fraction.

20. Find the area of the largest regular octagon that can be inscribed in a square of side length 12.

21. Consider the domain of the function $f(x) = \dfrac{|x| + 4}{|x| - 4}$. How many real numbers are not in the domain?

22. How many terms does the arithmetic sequence $5, 8, 11, \ldots, 3k + 20$ have? Express your answer in terms of k.

23. A knight travels from one corner of a standard (8 x 8) chessboard to the corner diagonally opposite. Which of the following could be the number of moves this journey took: 4, 7, 11, 18, 29?

24. A number is selected randomly from the first 12 even numbers. What is the probability that the number is not divisible by 3 or 4?

25. Five points are spaced evenly around a circle. How many polygons can be made with some (or all) of these points as vertices?

26. If $\{t_n\}$ is a geometric sequence with $t_1 + t_2 + t_3 + t_4 + t_5 = 44$ and $t_2 + t_3 + t_4 + t_5 + t_6 = 132$, then what is the value of t_3? Express your answer as a common fraction.

27. Find the sum of the distinct solutions to the equation $\frac{x^3 - 2x^2 + x}{x - 1} = 0$.

28. Find the volume of the largest regular tetrahedron that can be inscribed in a cube of side length 12.

29. Define the *power factorial* of n to be $P_f(n) = 1^1 \cdot 2^2 \cdots n^n$. Compute the largest integer n such that 3^n divides $P_f(81)$.

30. A sequence is defined by the rule $a_{n+2} = 2a_{n+1} + xa_n$. If $a_1 = 2$, $a_2 = 5$, and $a_3 = 14$, then what is a_4?

Target Test
Round 11512

Name: _____

Grade: _____

School: _____

Score: #1 _____ Scorer's Initials _____

Score: #2 _____ Scorer's Initials _____

1. What is the units digit of (416 - 211)(312 + 73)?

1.

2. The side length of a cube is increased by 30%. By what percent is the surface area increased?

2.

Target Test
Round 11512

Name: _____

Grade: _____

School: _____

---

place ID sticker inside this box

Score: #3 _____ Scorer's Initials _____

Score: #4 _____ Scorer's Initials _____

---

3. Evaluate $(2 + 4 + 6 + \cdots + 90) - (1 + 3 + 5 + \cdots + 89)$.

3.

4. An ant walks completely along the diagonal of a 5 by 7 rectangular grid (5 unit squares along the width, 7 along the length). How many of the 35 squares in the grid does the ant pass through?

4.

Target Test
Round 11512

5. Qings book "Functions" originally had 48 pages (counting each front and each back as a separate page). However, one of the 24 sheets, containing pages n and $n + 1$, was ripped out. The sum of her page numbers is now 1117. Find n.

5.

6. You are at a conference attended by mathematicians and philosophers. Your spies have told you that 20% of the mathematicians and 40% of the philosophers attending are evil. After some observation, you conclude that there are 2 evil philosophers present, and 25% of the total number of people present are evil. How many evil mathematicians are attending the conference?

6.

Name: _____

Grade: _____

School: _____

place ID sticker inside this box

Score: #7 _____ Scorer's Initials _____

Score: #8 _____ Scorer's Initials _____

7. The nth term of a sequence of positive integers, (a_n), is the nth positive integer with an odd number of positive divisors. For example, $a_1 = 1$ and $a_2 = 4$. Compute a_{25}.

7.

8. In how many ways can 8 identical white balls and 3 identical black balls be placed in a line such that no two black balls are adjacent to each other?

8.

Team Test
Round 11512

School/Team:

Score: #1 _____ Scorer's Initials _____

Score: #2 _____ Scorer's Initials _____

name or ID sticker goes in this box

name or ID sticker goes in this box

name or ID sticker goes in this box

name or ID sticker goes in this box

name or ID sticker goes in this box

name or ID sticker goes in this box

1.

2.

3.

4.

5.

6.

7.

8.

9.

10.

1. If $\left(3^3\right)^{3^{-3}} = 3^x$, find x.

2. Find the smallest integer n such that both $6n - 1$ and $6n + 1$ are composite.

3. Sally the Surveyor, strolling along the beach, pauses to admire a lighthouse. The structure is 100 feet tall and Sally knows that her eyes are exactly 5 feet above the ground. Whipping out her trusty antique astrolabe, she measures a 30° angle from her eyes to the top of the lighthouse. Several minutes later, she looks up and notices that the lighthouse seems significantly closer. This time she measures a 45° angle to its top. She suspects it is stalking her, but performs some calculations to be sure. How many feet has the lighthouse moved in her direction? Round your answer to the nearest integer.

4. If $i = \sqrt{-1}$, evaluate $i^0 + i^2 + \cdots + i^{50}$.

5. How many real solutions does the equation $|x^2 - 64| = 49$ have?

6. Compute the number of integer ordered triples (a, b, c) such that $a^2 + b^2 + c^2 = 34$.

7. A regular polygon has n sides and m diagonals. If $n + m = 28$, find n.

8. Let f be a function such that $f(ab) = f(a + b)$ for all real a and b. Given that $f(2014) = 1$, compute $f(1) + f(2) + \cdots + f(2014)$.

9. Let $p(x) = x^2 + 6x + 4$. If r and s are the roots of p, compute the value of $\frac{r}{s} + \frac{s}{r}$.

10. Sandeep has 4 songs that he gives to a DJ. He wants the songs to be played in a certain order, except he does not tell the DJ the order he wants. If the DJ plays the 4 songs in random order, what is the probability that at least one of the songs plays when it is supposed to? Express your answer as a common fraction.

1. There are eleven teams in a football league. Each team plays each other team once. How many games are played in all?

2. A quadrilateral has its vertices chosen from a 4 by 7 grid of points. What is the area of the largest possible quadrilateral that satisfies this condition?

3. What is the minimum value of $x^2 - 6x + 18$?

4. If 2 adjacent sides of a parallelogram have lengths of 6 and 10 and the angle between them is 60 degrees, what is the area of the parallelogram?

5. Box A has 1 red and 2 blue marbles, box B has 1 blue and 2 green marbles, and box C has 1 green and 2 red marbles. If Jane randomly chooses 1 marble from each box, what is the probability that she chooses one of each color? Express your answer as a common fraction.

6. If two square numbers have a difference of 49, what is the largest possible sum of those square numbers?

7. What is the largest integer x for which $\frac{1}{x}$ is larger than $\frac{8}{61}$?

8. Express as a decimal: $6 \times 100 + 3 \times 1 + \frac{7}{10}$.

9. What is the probability of getting exactly five heads when flipping six coins? Express your answer as a common fraction.

10. A cube with side length 7 is glued onto a cube with side length 9. What is the minimum possible surface area of this figure?

11. Two prime numbers have a sum of 150. What is the largest possible value of their difference?

12. How many 2-digit numbers are equal to 3 times the sum of their digits?

13. What is the sum of all integers between 17 and 53, inclusive?

14. Find the remainder when 7^{100} is divided by 343.

15. How many ordered pairs of integers (x, y) satisfy $\frac{1}{x} + \frac{1}{y} = \frac{1}{5}$?

16. Simplifiy: 63×33.

17. How diagonals are there in a regular hexagon?

18. A taxi charges \$2.40 plus \$0.25 per eighth of a mile. If two passengers need to travel 4 miles together and they want to split the cost of the taxi evenly, how much does each passenger pay? Express your answer in dollars and cents.

19. It takes a worker three-fifths of an hour to do one-fifth of a job. At this rate, how many hours will it take the worker to do the whole job?

20. Given that $a^b = 81$ and a and b are both integers, what is the smallest possible value of a?

21. Find the range of the list 37, 8, -15, 3, 18.

22. Two intersecting lines form an angle of 119 degrees at their intersection. What is the degree measure of the other angle the intersecting lines form?

23. Find the sum of the positive integer divisors of 28.

24. How many elements are in the intersection of $\{1 ; 5 ; 7 ; 2 ; 8 ; 6\}$ and $\{ 3 ; 1 ; 2 ; 8 ; 9 ; 12 ; 5 ; 6\}$?

25. James was bored so he counted cars for 4 hours. For every hour after the first, he counted twice as many cars as the hour before. If he counted a total of 660 cars, how many cars did he count during the 4th hour?

26. Evaluate: 11^4.

27. If 3 faces of a rectangular prism have an area of 42, 72, and 84 square units, what is the volume of the rectangular prism in cubic units?

28. What is the area of the quadrilateral with vertices at (2, 5), (6, 2), (2, -3), and (0, 2)?

29. If $4x + 9 = 53$, what is $6x + 4$?

30. Sally has 24 dollars to spend on pencils, which cost 3 dollars, and pens, which cost 4 dollars. How many combinations of pencils and pens can Sally buy, if she must spend all of her money?

31. How many different ways can all the letters of the word FOOTBALL be rearranged?

32. If four fair six-sided dice are rolled, what is the probability that the sum on the four dice is even? Express your answer as a common fraction.

33. N is an integer greater than 6, and when 201 is divided by N, the remainder is 6. For how many distinct positive integers N is this statement true?

34. If the average of 7 positive integers is 9, what is the maximum possible range of those integers?

35. x is a positive integer. If x is 14 times as large as y and $x - y = 715$, what is x?

36. 30% of what number is 45% of 78?

37. Points A, B, C, D lie on a line in that order. If $AC = 21$, $BD = 30$, and $AD = 45$, what is BC?

38. How many sides does a regular polygon have if its interior angles have a measure of 170 degrees?

39. How many noncongruent rectangles with integer side lengths have an area of 40?

40. If $3x^2 - 17x + 24 = 0$, what is the sum of the values for x? Express as a common fraction.

41. What is the surface area of a cone with a base radius of 7 and a height of 24? Express your answer in terms of π.

42. If a person runs 5 miles per hour, how many feet would they travel every 15 seconds?

43. What is the sum of 5 fives, 6 sixes, and 7 sevens?

44. If $x = 3$ and $y = \frac{1}{3}$, what is the value of $\frac{xy}{6} + 6y$? Express your answer as a common fraction.

45. If the arithmetic and geometric means of two integers are 65 and 63, respectively, what is the positive difference between the two integers?

46. If $x + y = 122$, $x + z = 34$, and $y + z = 70$, what is the value of $x + y + z$?

47. What is the y-coordinate of the lowest point of the parabola $y = x^2 - 6x - 18$?

48. What is the smallest composite number with no prime factor less than 13?

49. If pens cost \$0.35 each or 4 for \$1.25, how many cents are saved on the purchase of 24 pens by buying them in sets of 4?

50. What is the area of a triangle with side lengths 13, 14, and 15?

51. If 10% of 20% of a number is 34, then what is the number?

52. How many multiples of 6 are greater than 400 but less than 800?

53. A sphere and a cylinder have the same volume, and the radius of the sphere is the same length as the base radius of the cylinder. What is the ratio of the height of the cylinder to the radius of the sphere? Express your answer as a common fraction.

54. Evaluate: 88×44.

55. A line segment has endpoints at (-5, -10) and (7, 14). What are the coordinates of the midpoint of the line segment?

56. How many diagonals does a nonagon have?

57. 24 is what percent of 60?

58. How many quarts are there in 5 gallons?

59. If you are allowed to use only pennies, dimes, and quarters to make a total of 65 cents, what is the maximum number of dimes you could have?

60. A rectangular box has a volume of three gallons. If all of its dimensions are tripled, then what is the volume of the new box in gallons?

61. For integers a and b, what is the smallest possible positive value of $15a + 20b$?

62. Compute: $\binom{8}{4}$.

63. How many seconds does it take the hour hand on a clock to rotate 15 degrees?

64. How many elements are in the intersection of {A, B, D, G, H} and {B, E, F, G, J}?

65. A right triangle with legs of length 6 and 11 is inscribed inside of a circle. What is the area of the circle? Express your answer as a common fraction in terms of π.

66. Two roots of the equation $3x^3 - 9x^2 + px + q = 0$ are 0 and 4. Find the third root of the equation.

67. It takes Ms Barker 45 minutes to drive to her school at 40 miles per hour. How many minutes will it take her to drive to her school and back if she drives an average of 50 miles per hour?

68. If five straight lines are drawn in a plane, what is the largest number of non-overlapping regions they can split the plane into?

69. 21 increased by three times a number is 78. What is the number?

70. How many ways can three points be chosen from the vertices of a regular octagon such that they form a right triangle when connected?

71. If the sum of the base and height of a triangle is 30, what is the maximum possible area of the triangle? Express your answer as a decimal.

72. What is the sum of the first 50 positive odd integers?

73. What is the greatest integer solution to $x^2 - 90 < 47$?

74. George drives at 60 miles per hour from his home to his school, and he drives at 90 miles per hour back home. What is the average speed at which he drove, in miles per hour?

75. Evaluate: 23×21.

76. What is the sum of the last 3 digits of $(\frac{1}{5})^{10}$ when written as a decimal?

77. The sum of 4 consecutive integers is 30. What is their product?

78. The measure of two exterior angles of a triangle are 112° and 93°. What is the third exterior angle measure, in degrees?

79. How many prime numbers are less than 40?

80. What is the product of all primes between 15 and 25?

Sprint Test

1. 961
2. -8.2
3. 256π
4. 8169178744
5. 224
6. 132
7. 1728
8. 2014
9. 36
10. 45
11. $\frac{256}{\pi}$
12. 2
13. 2
14. ($) 26500
15. 110.4
16. 250
17. 2
18. 8
19. $\frac{-3}{4}$
20. $288\sqrt{2} - 288$
21. 2
22. $k + 6$
23. 18
24. $\frac{1}{3}$
25. 16
26. $\frac{36}{11}$
27. 0
28. 576
29. 1782
30. 38

Target Test

1. 5
2. 69
3. 45
4. 11
5. 29
6. 3
7. 625
8. 84

Team Test

1. $\frac{1}{9}$
2. 20
3. 70
4. 0
5. 4
6. 48
7. 8
8. 2014
9. 7
10. $\frac{5}{8}$

Countdown

1. 55
2. 18
3. 9
4. $30\sqrt{3}$
5. $\frac{1}{3}$
6. 1201
7. 7
8. 603.7
9. $\frac{3}{32}$
10. 682
11. 128
12. 1
13. 1295
14. 0
15. 5
16. 2079
17. 9
18. $5.20
19. 3
20. -9
21. 52
22. 61
23. 56
24. 5
25. 352
26. 14641

27. 504
28. 24
29. 70
30. 3
31. 10080
32. $\frac{1}{2}$
33. 5
34. 56
35. 770
36. 117
37. 6
38. 36
39. 4
40. $\frac{17}{3}$
41. 224π
42. 110
43. 110
44. $\frac{13}{6}$
45. 32
46. 113
47. -27
48. 221
49. 90
50. 84
51. 1700
52. 67
53. $\frac{4}{3}$

54. 3872
55. (1,2)
56. 27
57. 40
58. 20
59. 6
60. 81
61. 5
62. 70
63. 1800
64. 2
65. $\frac{157\pi}{4}$
66. -1
67. 72
68. 16
69. 19
70. 20
71. 112.5
72. 2500
73. 11
74. 72
75. 483
76. 6
77. 3024
78. 155
79. 12
80. 7429

Sprint Test Solutions

1. $31^2 = 961$ and $32^2 = 1024$, so the largest square less than 1000 is 961.

2. If $3x + 14 = -7x - 68$, then $10x = -82$ and $x = -8.2$.

3. If the circumference is 32π, the diameter is 32 and the radius is 16. This gives us an area of $\pi r^2 = 16^2 \pi = 256\pi$.

4. The computations are tedious to carry out, but there's not much that can be done to shorten this one. You might want to consider this as $(2000 + 14)^3$ and expand it to $2000^3 + 3 \cdot 2000^2 \cdot 14 + 3 \cdot 2000 \cdot 14^2 + 14^3$.

5. Use order of operations. This is $(1 + 2 \cdot 81) - (4 - 5 \cdot 13) = (1 + 162) - (4 - 65) = 163 - (-61) = 224$.

6. To choose the mayor there are 12 possible candidates. Once the mayor is chosen there are 11 possible candidates for vice-mayor. Thus there are a total of $12 \times 11 = 132$ possible combinations.

7. $12 \times 12 \times 12 = 1728$

8. 2014 factors into $2 \cdot 19 \cdot 53$, so the product of the prime factors is still 2014.

9. There are 8 that start with 1 (units digit can be 2 through 9), 7 that start with 2, and so on, ending with 1 that starts with 8 (89). Just add the integers from 1 to 8 to get the answer.

10. There is 1 that starts with 1 (10), 2 that start with 2 (21 and 20), and so on, ending with 9 that starts with 9. Just add the integers from 1 to 9 to get the answer.

11. If the circumference is 32, the diameter is $\frac{32}{\pi}$ and the radius is $\frac{16}{\pi}$. This gives us an area of $\pi r^2 = \frac{256}{\pi}$.

12. P lies on the sphere, so $OP = 2$.

13. Square both sides to obtain $x^2 = 2 + x$, or $x^2 - x - 2 = 0$, which factors as $(x - 2)(x + 1) = 0$.

The solutions to this are $x = 2$ and $x = -1$, but $x = -1$ is extraneous since $\sqrt{2 + (-1)} \neq -1$.

14. Simple Interest = principal $\cdot$ rate $\cdot$ time. The total interest on the loan is thus $\$20000 \cdot .065 \cdot 5 = \$6500$. The total amount owed is principal plus interest, or $\$26500$.

15. Assuming Kaylene keeps her promise, she will cover $\frac{\$26500}{2} = \$13250$ of the debt, leaving the other $\$13250$ for Utnapishtim. At $\$10$ per month, it will take him 1325 months, or 110.4 years, to pay off the wrecked van. Let us hope, for his sake, that his income increases after he finishes college, and that he never again tries to act out the books he reads about anthropomorphized racoons racing large vehicles around the countryside.

16. Horizontally (east to west), Rachel and Michael end up being separated by $80 + 100 + 60 = 240$ meters. Vertically, they are separated by $(50 - 30) + 50 = 70$ meters. Then, by Pythagorean Theorem, they end separated by $\sqrt{240^2 + 70^2} = 250$ meters.

17. By Heron's formula, the area of the triangle is 84. The area is also equal to $\frac{1}{2}(AH)(BC)$, so AH must equal 12. Then by the Pythagorean Theorem, $BH = \sqrt{13^2 - 12^2} = 5$. Also, $BM = 7$, so $MH = BM - BH = 2$.

18. $p^2qr + pq^2r + pqr^2 = (pqr)(p + q + r)$, so we are looking for the product of the roots times the sum of the roots. The product is -4 and the sum is -2.

19. $\frac{1}{p} + \frac{1}{q} + \frac{1}{r} = \frac{pq + pr + qr}{pqr}$, so we are looking for the sum of the roots two at a time divided by the product of the roots. The sum of the roots two at a time is 3, and the product is -4.

20. To find the area of the octagon, we just subtract from the area of the square (144) the area of the four triangles that are cut off the corners. Each triangle has hypotenuse x, where x is the side length of the octagon. Each side of the square consists of a side length of the oc-

tagon (x) surrounded on either side by the leg of one of the triangles mentioned above ($\frac{x}{\sqrt{2}}$). These pieces add to 12, giving us $x + 2\frac{x}{\sqrt{2}} = 12$ or $x(1 + \sqrt{2}) = 12$. Solving for x we get $x = \frac{12}{1+\sqrt{2}} = 12\sqrt{2} - 12$. Rearrange the triangles to form a square with side length x, and the area is $x^2 = 432 - 288\sqrt{2}$. Subtract this from 144 to get the final answer.

21. The only real numbers not in the domain are those with $|x| - 4 = 0$, so 4 and -4.

22. The common difference of this sequence is 3. Then if 5 is the first term, the nth term is $5 + 3(n-1)$. Setting this equal to $3k + 20$ gives $3(n-1) = 3k + 15$, or $n - 1 = k + 5$, so $n = k + 6$, and this is the number of terms.

23. Note that on a chessboard given the standard coloring, a knight will always move from a black square to a white square or from a white square to a black square, switching colors with each move. Note also that the opposite corners of a chessboard have the same color. The knight returns to its original color every other move, so it must take an even number of moves to reach the opposite corner. It is however impossible to complete the journey in 4 moves, so 18 is the only choice that works here.

24. Of the first 12 even numbers, half are divisible by 4. The 6 remaining are 2, 6, 10, 14, 18, and 22. Two of these are divisible by 3, leaving 4 out of 12, so the probability is $\frac{1}{3}$.

25. Such a polygon must have 3, 4, or 5 vertices. Once the vertices are chosen, there is only one way to connect them to form a polygon. Thus the number of polygons is $\binom{5}{3} + \binom{5}{4} + \binom{5}{5} = 10 + 5 + 1 = 16$.

26. Let r be the common ratio of the sequence. Since $t_2 = rt_1$, $t_3 = rt_2$, and so forth, $t_2 + t_3 + t_4 + t_5 + t_6 = r(t_1 + t_2 + t_3 + t_4 + t_5)$, so

$r = \frac{132}{44} = 3$. Let $x = t_3$. Then $t_1 + t_2 + t_3 + t_4 + t_5 = \frac{1}{9}x + \frac{1}{3}x + x + 3x + 9x$, so $\frac{121}{9}x = 44$, from which $x = \frac{9 \cdot 44}{121} = \frac{36}{11}$.

27. Factor the numerator of the left side of the equation: $\frac{x(x-1)(x-1)}{x-1} = 0$. Canceling yields $x(x - 1) = 0$, so $x = 0$ or $x = 1$. But note that the original equation has $x - 1$ in the denominator, so x cannot be 1. Thus $x = 0$ is the only solution.

28. This tetrahedron will have four vertices that coincide with vertices of the cube, and its edges will lie on faces of the cube. Each edge will have length $12\sqrt{2}$. The base is just an equilateral triangle with side length $12\sqrt{2}$, which gives us an area of $\frac{s^2\sqrt{3}}{4} = 72\sqrt{3}$. Now we multiply this by one third of the height. The height will pass through the center of the base, the distance of which from a base vertex is $\frac{2}{3}$ of the altitude of the base. The base altitude is $6\sqrt{6}$, so the center is $4\sqrt{6}$ from a vertex. This length forms the short leg of a right triangle with the other leg being the height we are looking for, and the hypotenuse being an edge of the tetrahedron. Now we can set up an equation: $(4\sqrt{6})^2 + h^2 = (12\sqrt{2})^2$. Simplifying, we get $96 + h^2 = 288$ or $h^2 = 192$. Thus $h = \sqrt{192} = 8\sqrt{3}$. Multiplying the area of the base times one third of the height gives us $72\sqrt{3} \cdot \frac{1}{3} \cdot 8\sqrt{3} = 576$.

29. If k is divisible by 3 once, then it contributes k factors of 3 to $P_f(81)$ from the k^k part. If it is divisible by 3 twice, then it contributes $2k$ factors of 3, and so on. Thus the number of factors of 3 in $P_f(81)$ is $(3 + 6 + 9 + ... + 81) + (9 + 18 + 27 + ... + 81) + (27 + 54 + 81) + 81$. This is $1134 + 405 + 162 + 81 = 1782$.

30. Let $n = 1$ in the given formula. Then we obtain $14 = 2 \cdot 5 + x \cdot 2$, so $x = 2$. Then $a_4 = 2 \cdot 14 + 2 \cdot 5 = 38$.

Target Test Solutions

1. $416 - 211 = 205$, and $312 + 73 = 385$. Both of these numbers end in a 5, and $5 \cdot 5 = 25$. Thus the units digit of their product is 5.

2. The new surface area is $1.3^2 = 1.69$ times as much as the original surface area, so our answer is 69.

3. There are 45 terms in each sum, and each term of the first sum is one more than each term of the second sum, so the answer is 45.

4. The ant must move 5 units up and 7 units over to reach the opposite corner. Each time it moves one unit up or one unit over, it enters a new square. Since 5 and 7 are relatively prime, these never happen at the same time. The exception is when the ant reaches the end of its journey (i.e. the last unit in each direction), when it does not enter a new square. Thus it enters a new square $4 + 6 = 10$ times. Add the square it starts in for a total of 11 squares that it passes through.

5. The original sum of the pages is $\frac{48 \cdot 49}{2} = 1176$. The difference between the original sum and the post-rip sum is $1176 - 1117 = 59$. Therefore, $n + (n+1) = 59$ and $n = 29$.

6. Call p the number of philosophers present. If two evil philosophers make up 40% of the philosophers attending the conference, then $\frac{40}{100} \cdot p = 2$. Simplifying and dividing we find that $p = 5$, so there are five philosophers at the conference. Then call e the number of evil mathematicians present. We know that only $20\% = \frac{20}{100} = \frac{1}{5}$ of the mathematicians present are evil, so there must be $5e$ total mathematicians at the conference. Then recall that 25% of the conference attendees are evil. There are 5 philosophers and $5e$ mathematicians for a total of $5 + 5e$ professors present, and 2 philosophers plus e mathematicians are evil, for a total of $2 + e$ evil professors. Thus $\frac{2+e}{5+5e} = \frac{25}{100}$, or cross-multiplying, $4e + 8 = 5e + 5$. Combining like terms, we find that $e = 3$, so there are 3 evil mathematicians at the conference.

7. If k is a positive integer that is *not* a perfect square, then the divisors of k come in pairs: if d is a divisor, then it is paired with $\frac{k}{d}$. If $k = n^2$, however, then n does not pair up in this way, so k has an odd number of divisors. Thus $a_n = n^2$, and $a_{25} = 625$.

8. The balls can be placed in any way, except that there must be a white ball between the first and second black balls, and a white ball between the second and third black balls. To account for this, remove two white balls, arrange the remaining 9 balls in any way, and insert the last two white balls in between black balls. There are $\binom{9}{3} = 84$ ways to do this.

Team Test Solutions

1. This is equal to $3^{3 \cdot 3^{-3}} = 3^{3^{-3+1}} = 3^{1/9}$.

2. Neither $6n-1$ nor $6n+1$ can be divisible by 2 or 3, so they must both be divisible by two or more primes (or the square of a prime) greater than 3. The first few such products of two primes are 35, 55, 65, 77, 85, 91, 95, 115, 119, and the first few such squares are 25, 49, 121. We're looking for two numbers in this list that are 2 apart, so the smallest solution is $6n - 1 = 119 = 17 \cdot 7$, $6n + 1 = 121 = 11^2$, and $n = 20$.

3. Sally's eyes are 5 feet off the ground and lighthouse is 100 feet tall, so the top of the lighthouse must be 95 feet higher than Sally's eyes. Sally draws a right triangle with her eyes as point A, 5 feet above the base of the lighthouse as point B, and the top of the lighthouse as point C. $\overline{AC}$ forms the hypotenuse. She has measured $\angle A$ at 30°. Recognizing that she has a 30°-60°-90° triangle, she realizes that $\overline{AB} = 95\sqrt{3} \approx 165$ feet. (It is actually 164.5448267... feet, but Sally rounds prematurely. This is a horrible habit to get into, but we will be merciful about judging her since she is on vaca-

tion and since, in this case, the early round-off does not affect the answer.) Using a similar method later for a second triangle DEF in which her eyes to the top of the lighthouse form the hypoteneuse $\overline{DF}$, she realizes that she has a 45°-45°-90° triangle in which sides $\overline{DE}$ and $\overline{EF}$ must be equal, meaning the lighthouse is now 95 feet away from her. The structure has moved 165 - 95 = 70 feet in a short time. Sadly, while Sally is working this all out, the lighthouse pounces and eats her, thus ruining her vacation. This is shocking behavior, of course, but lighthouses are inherently evil.

4. For any integer n, $i^{4n} = (i^4)^n = 1$ and $i^{4n+2} = i^{4n} \cdot i^2 = -1$. In the desired sum, there are an equal number (13) of i^{4n} terms and i^{4n+2} terms, so everything cancels out, leaving an answer of 0.

5. $x^2 - 64$ must equal 49 or -49, so x^2 is either $64+49 = 113$ or $64-49 = 15$. Thus $x = \pm\sqrt{113}$ or $x = \pm\sqrt{15}$.

6. If $a = 0$, then we can have the ordered triple $(0, \pm3, \pm5)$. We can choose the signs in 2^2 ways and arrange the numbers in 3! ways, so the total number of ordered triples for this case is 24. For $a = 1, 2$ there are no solutions. For $a = 3$, we can have $(\pm3, \pm3, \pm4)$. In this case, we can choose signs in 2^3 ways and choose which of the three numbers is ±4 in 3 ways, for a total of 24 ordered triples. For $a = 4, 5$, we get solutions already counted. Our total is $24 + 24 = 48$.

7. The set of all sides and diagonals of an n-sided polygon is simply the set of all lines connecting its n vertices. One line connects each pair of vertices, so there are $\binom{n}{2} = \frac{n(n-1)}{2}$ such lines. Thus $\frac{n(n-1)}{2} = 28$, and multiplying and moving terms to the same side gives $n^2 - n - 56 = 0$. Factor this expression to find that $(n - 8)(n + 7) = 0$, so $n = 8$ or $n = -7$. Since n must be positive, $n = 8$.

8. Note that $f(2014) = f(0+2014) = f(0 \cdot 2014) = f(0)$. By the same argument, for any real a we have $f(a) = f(a + 0) = f(0)$. So the function is constant for all real values, and since one of the values is 1, the desired sum is 2014.

9. Note that $\frac{r}{s} + \frac{s}{r} = \frac{r^2+s^2}{rs}$. $p(x)$ must factor as $(x - r)(x - s)$, and expanding this out, we find that $r + s = -6$ and $rs = 4$. Thus $r^2 + s^2 = (r + s)^2 - 2rs = 28$, so our answer is $\frac{28}{4} = 7$.

10. Number the songs 1 through 4. There are 24 ways to arrange the songs; we will figure out how many of these ways do NOT have any song in the correct place. There are 3 ways to choose where song 1 ends up; suppose it ends up in position n. If song n ends in position 1, then the other two must also swap places. This gives 3 ways to arrange the songs. On the other hand, if song n ends in position m (with $m \neq 1$), then song m must wind up in the remaining position, and the song originally in that position must wind up in position 1. In this case, there are 3 choices for n and 2 choices for m, for a total of 6. Thus the probability no song stays in its correct place is $\frac{9}{24} = \frac{3}{8}$, so the probability that this will not happen is $\frac{5}{8}$.

Sprint Test
Round 11513

Name: _____

Grade: _____

School: _____

place ID sticker inside this box

Score: #1 _____ Scorer's Initials _____

Score: #2 _____ Scorer's Initials _____

1.	2.	3.	4.	5.
6.	7.	8.	9.	10.
11.	12.	13.	14.	15.
16.	17.	18.	19.	20.
21.	22.	23.	24.	25.
26.	27.	28.	29.	30.

1. A 120mm stick is snapped into 2 pieces, with one piece being 4 times as long as the other. How long is the longer piece, in mm?

2. Two prime numbers have a difference of 15. Compute their product.

3. What is $3 \cdot 4 - 8 \div 2$?

4. What is the sum of the first 100 even integers?

5. A menu has 3 appetizers, 5 main dishes, and 4 desserts. How many different three-course meals can be made from this menu, if each meal must consist of one appetizer, one main dish, and one dessert?

6. What is the area of a circle with diameter $\frac{8}{\sqrt{\pi}}$?

7. Compute 11^5.

8. What is the absolute value of the difference of the roots of $x^2 + 9x - 36$?

9. How many 3-digit numbers contain only even digits?

10. The area of a square with side length 6 is numerically equal to half the perimeter of a regular hexagon. If the area of the regular hexagon can be expressed as $a\sqrt{b}$ in simplest radical form, find $a + b$.

11. One third of John's age is the same as the square root of $\frac{4}{3}$ of his age. How old is John?

12. A triangle has sides of length 13, 14, and 15. Compute the length of the altitude to the side of length 14.

13. The mathleague problem writing team has a $\frac{1}{3}$ chance of winning any given math contest. What is the probability that they win at least one of three contests that they participate in?

14. On a small isolated island, there are four letters in the alphabet. How many possible words can the islanders make, if their words are no longer than four letters?

15. A fair six-sided die and a fair twelve-sided die are both rolled. What is the probability that the sum of the numbers rolled is at most 6? Express your answer as a common fraction.

16. If $\sqrt[3]{a} = \sqrt{b} = c$ and a, b, and c are positive integers at most 1000000, what is the largest possible value of $a + b + c$?

17. In rectangle ABCD, AB=8 and BC=6. If E is the midpoint of AB and F is the midpoint of AC, what is the area of triangle DEF?

18. Let A be the area of a triangle with side lengths 10, 13, and 13. Let B be the area of a triangle with sides 13, 13, and 24. Compute $A - B$.

19. How many integers are there between $-8\sqrt{11}$ and $8\sqrt{11}$?

20. An equilateral triangle is inscribed in a circle of radius one. A semicircle is then inscribed in one of the three regions outside the triangle but inside the circle such that the semicircles base borders a side of the triangle. What is the largest possible area of the semicircle? Express your answer as a common fraction in terms of π.

21. Bob writes the numbers from 1 to 49 in base 7 on a chalkboard. What is the sum of all of the digits he wrote down? Express your answer in base 10.

22. A positive integer has 3 digits in base 7 and 4 digits in base 3. How many possible values are there for the number?

23. A five digit number satisfies the following conditions: the first and last digits are different, the second digit is a nonzero multiple of 3, and the third digit and the first digit differ by no more than 1. How many possible numbers are there?

24. 10 indistiguishable apples are to be distributed among 5 distinguishable people with nobody getting more than 3 and everybody receiving at least 1. How many ways can this be done?

25. What are the last two digits of 2014^{2014}?

26. Let $f(x) = 8x - 6$ and $g(x) = 2x^2 - 128$, and let $h(x) = f(x) - g(x)$. Compute the sum of the squares of the roots of $h(x)$.

27. There is an ordered triple of positive integers (a, b, c) that satisfies $(a + b)(b + c) = 91$ and $(a + b)(a + c) = 70$. Compute $ab + bc + ca$.

28. If $x = 2 - \sqrt{3}$, compute the value of $x^4 + 1/x^4$.

29. If a and b are positive real numbers that satisfy the equations $b - a^2 = 3$ and $a^4 + b^2 = 17$, compute b.

30. What is the smallest prime factor of $\frac{5^{35} - 1}{4}$?

Target Test
Round 11513

Name: _____

Grade: _____

School: _____

Score: #1 _____ Scorer's Initials _____

Score: #2 _____ Scorer's Initials _____

1. Rasputin the Reindeer and 5 elves form Santa's ground crew: they maintain the sleigh, check the weather, update Santa's flight plan, and so forth. When Mrs. Claus makes Christmas cookies for the ground crew, she gives Rasputin gets $\frac{1}{4}$ of the cookies. The other 5 elves each get only $\frac{1}{5}$ of the remaining cookies. The total number of cookies eaten by Rasputin and one of the ground crew elves is 24. What was the total number of cookies originally?

1. _____

2. A triangle has sides of length 12, 16, and 20. Compute its area.

2. _____

Target Test
Round 11513

Name: _____

Grade: _____

School: _____

place ID sticker inside this box

Score: #3 _____ Scorer's Initials _____

Score: #4 _____ Scorer's Initials _____

3. Alex has a 2 liter solution that is 5% acid. How many liters of pure acid would he have to add to the solution to make the overall solution 10% acid? Express your answer as a common fraction.

3. _____

4. How many consecutive zeros occur at the end of 50! ?

4. _____

Name: _____

Grade: _____

School: _____

place ID sticker inside this box

Score: #5 _____ Scorer's Initials _____

Score: #6 _____ Scorer's Initials _____

5. A number is written as 2014 when expressed in base 8. Express this number in base 10.

5.

6. Bob randomly takes six steps of equal length, each either forward or backward, with equal probability. What is the probability that Bob ends within one step of his starting point? Express your answer as a common fraction.

6.

Name: _____

Grade: _____

School: _____

place ID sticker inside this box

Score: #7 _____ Scorer's Initials _____

Score: #8 _____ Scorer's Initials _____

7. How many of the positive divisors of 2015 are divisible by 5?

7.

8. Handong's house is located at the origin, and his swim meet will be at the nearest pool, located at $(2, 5)$. However, before going to the pool, he wants to stop at the river defined by the line $y = 8$. If the length of the shortest path that Handong can take from his house to the swim meet can be expressed as $\sqrt{k}$ for some positive integer k, compute k.

8.

Team Test
Round 11513

School/ Team:

Score: #1 _____ Scorer's Initials _____

Score: #2 _____ Scorer's Initials _____

name or ID sticker goes in this box	name or ID sticker goes in this box
name or ID sticker goes in this box	name or ID sticker goes in this box
name or ID sticker goes in this box	name or ID sticker goes in this box

1.

2.

3.

4.

5.

6.

7.

8.

9.

10.

1. What is the smallest positive integer that leaves a remainder of 4 when divided by 5, a remainder of 5 when divided by 6, and a remainder of 6 when divided by 7?

2. A point is randomly chosen from a square of side length 2 meters. What is the probability that the point is within 1 meter of the center of the square?

3. What is the surface area of a hemisphere with radius 7?

4. Positive real numbers a and b satisfy $a + \frac{1}{b} = 7$ and $b + \frac{1}{a} = 5$. What is the value of $ab + \frac{1}{ab}$?

5. Compute the tens digit of the sum $(1!)^2 + (2!)^2 + \ldots + (2014!)^2$. $(n! = 1 \cdot 2 \cdot 3 \cdot \ldots \cdot n)$

6. Compute the remainder when 7^{42} is divided by 100.

7. If a and b are positive integers that satisfy $\frac{18}{37} = \frac{1}{a + \frac{1}{b}}$, compute $a + b$.

8. Let $x = 8640$. If m is the number of factors of x, and n is the number of factors of $9x$, compute the value of $\frac{m}{n}$ as a common fraction.

9. A right triangle has area 9 and hypotenuse 8. What is its perimeter?

10. Richard, Michael, and Carolyn are all playing a game. They each take turns rolling a fair 6-sided die. The first person to roll a 6 wins. If Carolyn rolls third, what is the probability that she does not win?

1. For a certain weekend, the probability that it rains on Saturday is $\frac{1}{3}$ and the probability that it rains on Sunday is $\frac{2}{5}$. If the probabilities are independent, what is the probability that it rains sometime during the weekend? Express your answer as a common fraction.

2. Sally writes the first 100 positive integers on a blackboard, then erases the factors of 75 and the multiples of 3. How many integers are left?

3. How many nonnegative integers less than 100 are divisible by 5?

4. Solve for x: $(x-1) + 2(x-2) + 3(x-3) = 40$

5. A car travels 152 miles on 8 gallons of gas. How many miles can it travel on 13 gallons of gas?

6. Compute: $\frac{51!}{48!}$

7. What is the y-coordinate of the y-intercept of the line that passes through the point $(6, 1)$ and has a slope of $\frac{2}{3}$?

8. How many ways are there to arrange the letters of the word POTATO?

9. The number 2436 is $\frac{4}{7}$ of another number. What is the other number?

10. The ratio of the measure of the three angles in a triangle is 4:5:7. What is the supplement of the smallest angle of the triangle, in degrees?

11. When the base 10 integer 616 is expressed in base 2, how many of its digits are 1?

12. What is the sum of the first 76 odd positive integers?

13. When a class is arranged in rows of 5, there are 2 students left over. When the class is arranged in rows of 6, there are 3 students left over. If the class has fewer than 40 students, how many students are in the class?

14. If the least common multiple of two positive integers is 36, what is the least possible sum of the two integers?

15. The price of a watch was increased by 35%. If the new price of the watch is $486, how many dollars did the watch originally cost?

16. a and b are positive integers that satisfy the equation $42a = 30b$. What is the least possible value of $a + b$?

17. A treasure map says that you need to move 19 feet north, 20 feet east, 11 feet south, and 26 feet west, to find the treasure. How many feet away from you is the treasure?

18. Ruth is three years older than Karen and four years younger than Alex. If the sum of Ruth's and Karen's ages is 29, how old is Alex?

19. How many positive integers less than 1000 are multiples of 11 and not multiples of 13?

20. Lori can mow an entire lawn in 3 hours. Christine can mow half of the same lawn in 4 hours. If Lori and Christine work together, how many hours will it take them to mow the entire lawn? Express your answer as a common fraction.

21. What is the product of the greatest common divisor and least common multiple of 30 and 42?

22. If the greatest common divisor of a and b is greater than 30, what is the least possible value of $a + b$?

23. A cube has edges with a length of 4 cm. What is the surface area of the cube, in cm^2?

24. How many integers between 24 and 48, inclusive, can be written as the difference of two perfect squares?

25. How many prime numbers less than 100 have digits that sum to 7?

26. If the area of an equilateral triangle is numerically equal to the triangle's perimeter, what is the side length of the triangle? Express your answer in simplest radical form.

27. A certain sponge absorbs 27% of the water in the container it is placed in. If the sponge absorbs 135 tablespoons of water in a container, how many tablespoons of water are left in the container after the sponge is removed?

28. Printing a book costs 5 cents per page plus 3 dollars for the cover. If Samuel has 7 dollars, how many pages are in the longest book that Samuel can afford to print?

29. A pair of coins are flipped simultaneously. If at least one coin lands on heads, what is the probability that both coins land on heads? Express your answer as a common fraction.

30. The sides of a right triangle are x, $x + 1$, and 5 units, where x is a positive integer. What is the sum of all possible areas of the right triangle?

31. If $x = 4$ and $7x + 10y = 13$, what is the value of y? Express your answer as a common fraction.

32. What is the smallest positive integer with exactly 6 positive divisors?

33. If the length of each side of a square is decreased by 20%, by what percent does the area of the square decrease?

34. Two concentric circles have radii of 16 cm and 34 cm. What is the length of a chord of the larger circle that is tangent to the smaller circle, in cm?

35. Two gallons of lemonade with 25% lemon juice and a gallon of lemonade with 19% lemon juice are mixed together. What percent of the mixture is lemon juice?

36. Sean flips 8 coins. What is the probability that he gets fewer than 2 heads or fewer than 2 tails? Express your answer as a common fraction.

37. What is the minimum value of $x^2 - 12x - 13$ over all real x?

38. A plane at an altitude of 0 meters begins ascending at a constant rate of 600 meters per minute. How many seconds will it take the plane to reach an altitude of 1000 meters?

39. A cone has a base radius of 6 cm and a slant height of 7 cm. What is the surface area of the cone, in cm^2? Express your answer in terms of π.

40. What is the mean of the set of numbers 42, 27, 26, 40, 35?

41. Point A is reflected across the line $y = x$, and then rotated 90 degrees clockwise around the origin to point B. If the coordinates of point A are (-7, -18), what are the coordinates of point B? Express your answer as an ordered pair.

42. Mary has 6 pairs of white socks, 4 pairs of black socks, 3 pairs of green socks, and 2 pairs of blue socks. What fraction of her socks are black?

43. If triangle ABC has an area of 48 cm^2 and AB$= 12$ cm, what is the height from vertex C of triangle ABC, in cm?

44. Compute $123 + 234 + 345 + 456 + 654 + 765 + 876 + 987$.

45. Dennis took a 60-question test and answered all but 18 of the problems correctly. What percentage of the problems did he answer correctly?

46. What is the sum of all integer values of x such that $|x^2 - 25|$ is a prime number?

47. For how many integers x is the value of $x^2 + 2x + 1$ between 20 and 40, inclusive?

48. Richard can run 132 feet in 7 seconds. At this rate, how many seconds will it take him to run a mile?

49. A pound of mixed nuts costs \$1.99. How many dollars does it cost to purchase 8 pounds of mixed nuts? Express your answer as a decimal.

50. Compute $\sqrt{99920016}$.

51. Compute $37 \cdot 30 + 37 \cdot 33 + 37 \cdot 36$.

52. A magazine subscription costs 6 dollars per month. At this rate, how many dollars will it cost to subscribe for 9 years?

53. The graphs of $y = -2x^2 + 9x - 2$ and $y = -29$ intersect at two points. What is the sum of the x-coordinates of these two points? Express your answer as a common fraction.

54. If the sum of two primes is 49, what is the greatest possible value of the product of those two primes?

55. Let $f(x) = 6x + 2$ and $g(x) = -2x + 3$. Compute the value of $f(g(3)) - g(f(-3))$.

56. Charlie has 8 marbles, each a different color. If one marble is red and another marble is blue, how many ways can Charlie choose 2 marbles without choosing both the red and blue marbles?

57. A square pyramid has base edges with a length of 5 cm and a height of 9 cm. What is the volume of the pyramid, in cm^3?

58. How many degrees does the minute hand of a clock move in 26 minutes?

59. Amy forgot the last digit of her friend's house number but remembers the rest of her friend's address. She also knows that the street her friend lives on only has even house numbers. How many doors does Amy need to knock on before she is guaranteed to knock on her friend's door?

60. A regular heptagon has the same perimeter as a regular hexagon with a side length of 14 cm. What is the side length of the heptagon, in cm?

61. If x and y are positive integers such that $x^2 - y^2 = 23$, what is the value of $x + y$?

62. If the sum of the first 11 terms of an arithmetic sequence is 143, what is the 6th term of the sequence?

63. A bike travels at a constant speed of 7 km/h. A car starts 108 km behind the bike and travels at a constant speed of 19 km/h. How far, in km, does the car travel before it catches up with the bike?

64. Robert purchases 15 stools and chairs. Each stool has 3 legs and each chair has 4 legs. If there are a total of 53 legs among the 15 stools and chairs, how many stools did Robert purchase?

65. If $2x + 6y = 14$ and $3x + y = 5$, what is the value of $x + y$?

66. If Cynthia turned 24 years old in 2010, in what year was she born?

67. Two fair six-sided dice are rolled. What is the probability that the sum of the two numbers showing is greater than 5 and less than 10? Express your answer as a common fraction.

68. The midpoints of the sides of a rectangle are connected to form a rhombus. If the rectangle has a length of 5 cm and a width of 8 cm, what is the area of the rhombus, in cm^2?

69. If the volume of a cube is $648\sqrt{3}$ cm^3, what is the length of the cube's interior diagonal, in cm?

70. What common fraction is 45% more than $\frac{4}{5}$?

71. An ice cream shop has 6 different flavors of ice cream. Rosemary wants to purchase a three scoop ice cream cone such that each scoop contains one flavor and no two scoops have the same flavor. How many different combinations of scoops can she get on her ice cream cone if the order of the scoops doesn't matter?

72. What is the remainder when 432987 is divided by 9?

73. How many cubic inches of wood are in a block of wood 2 inches long, 1.5 inches wide, and 1 foot tall?

74. If the legs of a right triangle have a length of 10 cm and 13 cm, what is the area of the right triangle, in cm^2?

75. The sum of an integer and its reciprocal is an integer. What is the value of the square of the integer?

76. What is the largest factor of 144 with exactly 4 positive factors?

77. A triangle has sides of length 10 cm, 24 cm, and 26 cm. What is the circumference of the circumcircle of the triangle, in cm? Express your answer in terms of π.

78. The operation # is defined as $a\#b = a^3 - b^2$. What is the value of $8\#(3\#5)$?

79. The equation of a circle is $(x - 2)^2 + (y + 2)^2 = 121$. What is the radius of the circle?

Countdown - Round 11513 - © 2014 mathleague.org

80. Compute $|3| - |-4| + |3 - (-4)|$.

Sprint Test

1. 96 (mm)
2. 34
3. 8
4. 10100
5. 60
6. 16
7. 161051
8. 15
9. 100
10. 219
11. 12
12. 12
13. $\frac{19}{27}$
14. 340
15. $\frac{5}{24}$
16. 1010100
17. 6
18. 0
19. 53
20. $\frac{\pi}{8}$
21. 295
22. 32
23. 7020
24. 51
25. 16
26. 138
27. 66
28. 194
29. 4
30. 11

Target Test

1. 60
2. 96
3. $\frac{1}{9}$ (liters)
4. 12
5. 1036
6. $\frac{5}{16}$
7. 4
8. 125

Team Test

1. 209
2. $\frac{\pi}{4}$
3. 147π
4. 33
5. 1
6. 49
7. 20
8. $\frac{2}{3}$
9. 18
10. $\frac{66}{91}$

Countdown

1. $\frac{3}{5}$
2. 64
3. 20
4. 9
5. 247 (miles)
6. 124950
7. -3
8. 180
9. 4263
10. 135(°)
11. 4
12. 5776
13. 27
14. 13
15. ($)360
16. 12
17. 10 (feet)
18. 20
19. 84
20. $\frac{24}{11}$ (hours)
21. 1260
22. 62
23. 96 (cm²)
24. 19
25. 3
26. $4\sqrt{3}$

27. 365 (tbsp)
28. 80 (pages)
29. $\frac{1}{3}$
30. 36
31. -$\frac{3}{2}$
32. 12
33. 36(%)
34. 60 (cm)
35. 23(%)
36. $\frac{9}{128}$
37. -49
38. 100 (seconds)
39. 78π (cm²)
40. 34
41. (-7, 18)
42. $\frac{4}{15}$
43. 8 (cm)
44. 4440
45. 70(%)
46. 0
47. 4
48. 280 (seconds)
49. ($)15.92
50. 9996
51. 3663
52. ($)648
53. $\frac{9}{2}$

54. 94
55. -51
56. 27
57. 75 (cm³)
58. 156(°)
59. 5
60. 12 (cm)
61. 23
62. 13
63. 171 (km)
64. 7
65. 3
66. 1986
67. $\frac{5}{9}$
68. 20 (cm²)
69. 18 (cm)
70. $\frac{29}{25}$
71. 20
72. 6
73. 36 (in³)
74. 65 (cm²)
75. 1
76. 8
77. 26π (cm)
78. 508
79. 11
80. 6

Sprint Test Solutions

1. The longer piece is $\frac{4}{5}$ of the original length.

2. Since their difference is odd, one of the primes must be 2. Then the other is 17, and our answer is 34.

3. $3 \cdot 4 - 8 \div 2 = 12 - 4 = 8$

4. This is equal to $2 + 4 + \ldots + 200 = 2 = (2 + 200) \cdot \frac{100}{2} = 202 \cdot 50 = 10100$.

5. The choices are all independent, so we just multiply the options together. $3 \cdot 5 \cdot 4 = 60$.

6. If the diameter is $\frac{8}{\sqrt{\pi}}$, the radius is $\frac{4}{\sqrt{\pi}}$. Squaring and multiplying by π gives us $\pi \frac{16}{\pi} = 16$.

7. $11^5 = 161051$.

8. $x^2 + 9x - 36 = (x + 12)(x - 3)$, so the roots are -12 and 3. The difference between these is 15.

9. We have 4 choices for the first digit (2, 4, 6, 8) and 5 choices for each of the last two digits (0, 2, 4, 6, 8). This gives us a total of $4 \cdot 5 \cdot 5 = 100$ numbers.

10. Let the side length of the hexagon be s. Then we have $\frac{6s}{2} = 36, s = 12$. Then, the area of the hexagon is $6 \cdot \frac{12^2 \sqrt{3}}{4} = 216\sqrt{3}$ and $a + b = 219$.

11. We have that $\frac{x}{3} = \sqrt{\frac{4x}{3}}$, so $x = 12$.

12. We can compute that the area is 84 (either using Heron's formula or splitting the triangle into two right triangles), so $(14h)/2 = 84$ and $h = 12$.

13. We use complementary probability. The probability that they lose all of three contests they participate in is $\left(\frac{2}{3}\right)^3 = \frac{8}{27}$, so our answer is $1 - \frac{8}{27} = \frac{19}{27}$.

14. We use casework. They can make 4^i words with i letters, so our answer is $4^1 + 4^2 + 4^3 + 4^4 = 340$.

15. The number of ways that a 2 can be rolled is 1. Similarly, a 3 can be rolled in 2 ways, a 4 can be rolled in 3 ways, a 5 can be rolled in 4 ways, and a 6 can be rolled in 5 ways. Then, the total number of ways to roll at most 6 is 15, so the answer is $\frac{15}{6 \cdot 12} = \frac{5}{24}$.

16. Because a is at most 1000000, c is at most $\sqrt[3]{1000000} = 100$. As c increases, a and b both increase, so the largest possible value of $a + b + c$ occurs at the maximum possible value for a, when $a = 1000000$, $c = 100$, and $b = 10000$, so $a + b + c = 1010100$.

17. Because EF connects the midpoints of AB and AC, EF is both half the length of BC and parallel to BC by SAS similarity. Because EF is parallel to BC and AE=EB, the altitude from D to EF is half the length of AB, so the $[\triangle DEF] = \frac{4 \cdot 3}{2} = 6$.

18. Both triangles are composed of two 5-12-13 right triangles. We have $A = \frac{bh}{2} = \frac{10 \cdot 12}{2} = 60$ and $B = \frac{bh}{2} = \frac{24 \cdot 5}{2} = 60$, so $A - B = 0$.

19. $(8\sqrt{11})^2 = 704$, so we want to count integers n with $n^2 < 704$. Since $26^2 < 704 < 27^2$, we need $-26 \leq n \leq 26$, and there are 53 such integers.

20. Because the base of the semicircle borders the triangle, the arc of the semicircle must be tangent to the big circle. Let the semicircle have radius r. Then, if we take the line segment from the center of the circle to the midpoint of the semicircle's base, it has length $1 - r$. We want to minimize $1 - r$, and this happens when the segment is the altitude from the center of the circle to a side of a triangle. This segment has length $\frac{1}{2}$, so the maximum possible value of r is $\frac{1}{2}$ and the area of the semicircle is $\left(\frac{1}{2}\right)^2 \cdot \frac{\pi}{2} = \frac{\pi}{8}$.

21. The units digit will take on the values 1,2,3,4,5,6,0 seven times each while the sevens digit takes the same values seven times each. The forty-nines digit takes on the value 1 once. So the total is $14(1 + 2 + 3 + 4 + 5 + 6) + 1 = 295$.

22. Call the number n. If n has three digits in base 7, then $7^2 \leq n \leq 7^3 - 1$. If n has four digits in base 3, then $3^3 \leq n \leq 3^4 - 1$. These ranges overlap with $49 \leq n \leq 80$, so the number of

possible values is $80 - 49 + 1 = 32$.

23. If the first digit is not 9, then there are 3 possibilities for the third digit. If it is 9, then the third digit can be either 8 or 9, for 2 possibilities. This means there are $8 \cdot 3 + 2 = 26$ possible combinations of the first and third digit. The second digit has 3 possibilities, the fourth digit has 10 possibilities, and the last digit can be any digit except the same as the first digit, for 9 possibilites. The total number of possibilities is $26 \cdot 3 \cdot 10 \cdot 9 = 7020$.

24. The ways that apples can be given to the five people is a permutation of $(2,2,2,2,2), (1,2,2,2,3)$, or $(1,1,2,3,3)$. For $(2,2,2,2,2)$, there is 1 way. For $(1,2,2,2,3)$, there are $\frac{5!}{3!} = 20$ ways. For $(1,1,2,3,3$, there are $\frac{5!}{2!2!} = 30$ ways. The total number of ways to distribute the apples is $1 + 20 + 30 = 51$.

25. Because we are only concerned about the last two digits, this is equivalent to $14^{2014} = 2^{2014}7^{2014}$. The last two digits of 7^4 are 01, so we can ignore as many copies of 7^4 as we have, leaving us with $2^{2014}7^2$. 2^2 and 2^{22} both end in 04, so in the same way the powers of 7 cycled in four, the powers of 2 cycle in twenty and we can ignore as many copies of 2^{20} as we have, leaving us with $2^{14}7^2 = 16384 \cdot 49$. The last two digits of this are 16.

26. We have that $h(x) = 8x - 6 - (2x^2 - 128) =$

$-2x^2 + 8x + 122$. Let the roots of $h(x)$ be r and s. By Vietas Theorem, $r + s = 4$ and $rs = -61$. Then $r^2 + 2rs + s^2 = 16$, so $r^2 + s^2 = 16 + 122 = 138$.

27. Note that $91 = 13 \cdot 7$, $70 = 10 \cdot 7$. Since $(a + b)$ appears in both products, it must be a positive integer dividing both 91 and 7, so $a + b = 7$ or $a + b = 1$. In the latter case, a and b cannot both be positive, so $a + b = 7$. Then $b + c = 13$ and $a + c = 10$. Subtract the last two equations to get $b - a = 3$, from which $b = 5$ and $a = 2$, and then $c = 8$. Then $ab + bc + ac = 66$.

28. After rationalizing the denominator, we can find that $x + 1/x = 2 - \sqrt{3} + 2 + \sqrt{3} = 4$. Then we can square that equation to find that $x^2 + 1/x^2 + 2 = 16$, so $x^2 + 1/x^2 = 14$. We can square once again and subtract two to find that $x^4 + 1/x^4 = 194$.

29. We have $a^2 = b - 3$, so $a^4 = b^2 - 6b + 9$. Then $2b^2 - 6b - 8 = 0$, which gives $2(b-4)(b+1) = 0$. Since b must be positive, $b = 4$.

30. Because $5^2 \equiv 1 \mod 8$, $5^{35} = (5^2)^{17} \cdot 5 \equiv 5 \mod 8$, so $5^{35} - 1 \equiv 4 \mod 8$ and $\frac{5^{35}-1}{4}$ is not divisible by 2. It is clearly not divisible by 5. We can calculate that the powers of 5 repeat period 2 mod 3, period 6 mod 7, and period 5 mod 11, so $\frac{5^{35}-1}{4} = \frac{(5^5)^7 - 1}{4} \equiv \frac{1-1}{4} = 0 \mod 11$, so 11 is the smallest prime factor.

Target Test Solutions

1. Let c be the original number of cookies. Rasputin eats $\frac{1}{4}c$ and the 1 elf eats $\frac{3}{4} \cdot \frac{1}{5}$ cookies. Together they eat $\frac{1}{4}c + \frac{3}{4} \cdot \frac{1}{5}$ cookies. Simplifying, we see that $\frac{2}{5}c = 24$ so $c = 60$. Thus Mrs. Claus provides 60 homemade Christmas cookies for the ground crew.

Rasputin eats 15 cookies, while each of the elves only get 9. It is no surprise that the disgruntled elves feel he is exercising undue influence at the North Pole. They plot to poison his milk. Then, after they succeed in getting rid of the unpopular reindeer, they hack into Santa's servers and change their statuses back to "nice" in the system.

2. This is a right triangle with legs 12 and 16, so the area is $\frac{1}{2} \cdot 12 \cdot 16 = 96$.

3. If the 2 liter solution is 5% acid, that means 100 ml is acid and 1900 ml something else. That 1900 ml will remain constant but now needs to comprise 90% of the total. The total amount of acid will be 10% of the total, or $\frac{1}{9}$ as much as the rest of the solution. $\frac{1}{9} \cdot 1900 = 211\frac{1}{9}$

ml. Subtracting the 100 ml we started with, we need to add $111\frac{1}{9}$ ml of acid, or $\frac{1}{9}$ of a liter.

4. Every time both a 2 and a 5 show up in the prime factorization of 50!, this contributes another trailing zero. There are far more 2's than 5's, so we need to find how many 5's are in the prime factorization of 50!. Every multiple of 5 (of which there are 10) contributes at least one 5, but the multiples of 25 (25 and 50) each contribute 2, for a total of 12.

5. The number 2014 in base 8 has two 512's, zero 64's, one 8, and four 1's. $2 \cdot 512 + 1 \cdot 8 + 4 \cdot 1 = 1036$.

6. There are $\frac{6!}{(3!)^2} = 20$ ways for Bob to end at his starting point. For Bob to end one unit forward of his starting point, he must have exactly one more forward move than backwards move.

Team Test Solutions

1. This number is 1 less than a multiple of 5, 1 less than a multiple of 6, and 1 less than a multiple of 7, so it is 1 less than a multiple of $5 \cdot 6 \cdot 7 = 210$. The smallest positive integer that is 1 less than a multiple of 210 is 209.

2. To find this probability, we first note that all points within 1 meter of the center of the square fall inside the square. So we need only to compute the area within 1 meter and divide that by the area of the square. The target area is a circle with radius 1, so its area is π, and the area of the square is 4.

3. To get the surface area, we take the surface area of half a sphere and then add the area of the flat side of the hemisphere. The full sphere would have surface area $4\pi r^2 = 196\pi$, so half of that would be 98π. The flat side of the hemisphere is a circle with radius 7, and its area is $\pi r^2 = 49\pi$. Adding these we get $98\pi + 49\pi = 147\pi$.

4. Multiply the equations to get $ab + 1 + 1 + \frac{1}{ab} = 35$, so our answer is $35 - 2 = 33$.

5. Note that if $n!$ is divisible by 10, then $(n!)^2$ is

However, two consecutive integers always have an odd sum and therefore cannot sum to 6. As a result, there is no way for Bob to be either one unit forward or backwards of his starting point, and there 20 ways total. Therefore the answer is $\frac{20}{64} = \frac{5}{16}$.

7. Since $2015 = 5 \cdot 13 \cdot 31$, any divisor of 2015 that is also divisible by 5 must be $5 \cdot k$, where k is either 1, 13, 31, or $13 \cdot 31$. There are 4 of these, so 4 of the positive divisors of 2015 are divisible by 5.

8. Reflect the point $(2, 5)$ across $y = 8$. Note that every path from the river to the pool corresponds to a path from the river to the reflected point. Now we want the shortest distance from the origin to the point $(2, 11)$, which is just $\sqrt{2^2 + 11^2} = \sqrt{125}$, so our answer is $k = 125$.

divisible by 100. Since $5! = 120$ and all factorials after that are divisible by 10, we just need to find the remainder when the sum of the first four terms of our sum is divided by 100. This is $1 + 4 + 36 + 576 = 617$, so our answer is 1.

6. Notice that mod 100, the powers of 7 cycle as 07, 49, 43, 01. Since $42 \equiv 2 \mod 4$, our answer is 49. Alternately, we can use Eulers theorem to reduce the problem to finding $7^2 \mod 100$ (which clearly is just 49).

7. Taking the reciprocal of both sides, we get $37/18 = a + 1/b$. Now $a = 2$, $b = 18$ satisfies the equation, so $a + b = 20$.

8. Note that $x = k \cdot 3^3$, and $9x = k \cdot 3^5$, where k is an integer not divisible by three. If p is the number of factors of k, then x has $4p$ factors, and $9x$ has $6p$ factors. Therefore $\frac{m}{n} = \frac{4p}{6p} = \frac{2}{3}$.

9. Let the legs of the triangle be a, b. Then $ab/2 = 9$ and $\sqrt{a^2 + b^2} = 8$. It follows that $a^2 + 2ab + b^2 = 100$, so $a + b = 10$ and the perimeter is $10 + 8 = 18$.

10. On any given turn, the probability that someone wins is $\frac{1}{6}$. Therefore the probability Car-

olyn wins on her first turn is $\left(\frac{5}{6}\right)^2\left(\frac{1}{6}\right)$, the probability that she wins on her second turn is just $\left(\frac{5}{6}\right)^5\left(\frac{1}{6}\right)$, et cetera. The probability that she wins is an infinite geometric series with first term $\frac{25}{216}$ and common ratio $\frac{125}{216}$. Therefore the probability that Carolyn wins is $\frac{25/216}{1-125/216} = \frac{25}{91}$, and the probability that she does not win is $\frac{66}{91}$.

Sprint Test
Round 11514

Name: _____

Grade: _____

School: _____

place ID sticker inside this box

Score: #1 _____ Scorer's Initials _____

Score: #2 _____ Scorer's Initials _____

1.	2.	3.	4.	5.
6.	7.	8.	9.	10.
11.	12.	13.	14.	15.
16.	17.	18.	19.	20.
21.	22.	23.	24.	25.
26.	27.	28.	29.	30.

1. Compute $\frac{10\cdot9\cdot8\cdot7}{4\cdot3\cdot2\cdot1}$.

2. If ♠$(x,y) = 2x + 3y$, compute ♠$(2, ♠(3,4))$.

3. Triangle ABC has $AB = 13$, $BC = 14$, and $AC = 15$. Point P is on AC such that $AP = CP$. Find the positive difference between the areas of triangles APB and CPB.

4. Three non-overlapping regular hexagons of side length 2 are joined to form a larger figure. What is the minimum possible perimeter of this figure?

5. Find the smallest five-digit positive factor of 20152015.

6. Compute $\frac{\sqrt{225}-\sqrt{144}}{\sqrt{225-144}}$.

7. A square has its sides tripled. By what percent does its area increase?

8. Compute the ratio of $\frac{2}{7}$ to $\frac{6}{13}$. Express your answer as a common fraction.

9. How many three-digit numbers can be formed from the digits $0, 1, 3, 5, 7, 8$ if each digit is to be used only once?

10. Jonathan has finished the fourth day of a seven day hiking trip. If he has completed $\frac{6}{11}$ of the trip's total distance of 209 km, how many km per day must he average for the remainder of the trip? Express your answer as a common fraction.

11. For how many integers x is $x^2 + 4 \leq 4x$?

12. What is the sum of the infinite geometric series $\frac{3}{5} + \frac{12}{25} + \frac{48}{125} + \dots$?

13. Compute the smallest possible value of $1 + x^4 + x^8$.

14. Find the area of a regular octagon with side length 6.

15. What is the sum of the squares of the roots of $x^2 + 9x + 14$?

16. A triangle is inscribed in a circle of radius 12. What is the largest possible area of this triangle?

17. For how many real values of x is $2 + \sqrt{x - 1} = -x$?

18. For any real number n, let $\lfloor n \rfloor$ represent the greatest integer less than or equal to n. Find the sum of all positive numbers n such that $n = \lfloor n \rfloor$ and $n < 10$.

19. What is the largest root of $x^3 + x^2 - 49x - 49$?

20. A quadrilateral has its vertices at $(0,0)$, $(0,1)$, $(3,4)$, and $(2,0)$. Find its area. Express your answer as a common fraction.

21. Compute $\sqrt[3]{61,629,875}$.

22. The number $20.15 \cdot 0.0005102$ can be expressed as $a \times 10^b$, where $1 \leq a < 10$ and b is an integer. Find the smallest integer greater than or equal to $a + b$.

23. A pyramid has a square base of side length 6 and equilateral triangles for its other faces. The surface area of the pyramid can be expressed as $a + b\sqrt{3}$. Compute $a + b$.

24. Compute the units digit of $1^2 + 2^2 + \cdots + 2014^2$.

25. In square $ABCD$ with side length 8, circle ω is drawn through points A and B and tangent to $\overline{CD}$. Compute the radius of ω.

26. If $i = \sqrt{-1}$, compute $(1 + i)^{16}$.

27. Let $N = 201520142013 \cdots 54321$ be the integer formed by writing the digits of each positive integer starting at 2015 and decreasing until we end at 1. Find the remainder when N is divided by 9.

28. Compute $\sqrt[5]{\left(\sqrt{4}^{\sqrt{125}}\right)^{\sqrt{5}}}$.

29. The numbers x, x^2, and $2x^3$ form a geometric progression in some order. Let the sum of all the possible values of x be S. Find the smallest positive integer greater than or equal to $4S$.

30. Evaluate $(\sin^2 18°)(\cos^2 27°) + \frac{1}{2}(\sin 36°)(\sin 54°) + (\sin^2 27°)(\cos^2 18°)$. Express your answer as a common fraction.

Name: _____

Grade: _____

School: _____

place ID sticker inside this box

Score: #1 _____   Scorer's Initials _____

Score: #2 _____   Scorer's Initials _____

1. How many five-digit numbers greater than 30000 can be formed from the digits $1, 2, 3, 4, 5$ if each digit is to be used only once and the number is divisible by 5?

1.

2. An isosceles right triangle has hypotenuse 10. What is its area?

2.

Name: _____

Grade: _____

School: _____

place ID sticker inside this box

Score: #3 _____ Scorer's Initials _____

Score: #4 _____ Scorer's Initials _____

3. Mr. DJ's pool is a 6 meter by 8 meter rectangle. He wants to install a 2.5 meter wide patio around it (square at the corners), and each square stone measures a half meter on a side. How many stones are required to build the patio?

3.

4. Let a and b be the smallest set of twin primes greater than 2015 (twin primes are primes that differ by 2). Find the sum of a and b.

4.

Name: _____

Grade: _____

School: _____

place ID sticker inside this box

Score: #5 _____ Scorer's Initials _____

Score: #6 _____ Scorer's Initials _____

5. Let $x = 2015$ and $y = 403$. Compute $\frac{x^3 \cdot y^2}{y^5} \cdot \frac{x}{y^4} \cdot \left(\frac{y^2}{x}\right)^3$.

5.

6. In how many ways can I distribute six indistinguishable candies to Jeff, Tim, and Steve if Jeff must get at least two candies?

6.

Target Test
Round 11514

Name: _____

Grade: _____

School: _____

place ID sticker inside this box

Score: #7 _____ Scorer's Initials _____

Score: #8 _____ Scorer's Initials _____

7. How many three letter words can be made from the letters of the word "BJORK"?

7.

8. Compute the following sum in simplest form:

$$\frac{1}{\sqrt{1}+\sqrt{2}} + \frac{1}{\sqrt{2}+\sqrt{3}} + \cdots + \frac{1}{\sqrt{99}+\sqrt{100}}.$$

8.

Team Test
Round 11514

School/
Team:

Score: #1 _____ Scorer's Initials _____

Score: #2 _____ Scorer's Initials _____

name or ID sticker goes in this box

name or ID sticker goes in this box

name or ID sticker goes in this box

name or ID sticker goes in this box

name or ID sticker goes in this box

name or ID sticker goes in this box

1.

2.

3.

4.

5.

6.

7.

8.

9.

10.

Team Test - Round 11514 - © 2015 mathleague.org

1. Mr. Omar has a square garden measuring 25 square meters. The garden is in the corner of his yard, which is a rectangle 2 meters wider and 3 meters longer than his garden. What is the perimeter of the area of his yard which is not part of the garden?

2. Brian made two 150-mile trips. His second trip took one hour less than his first trip, and the total time for both trips was 11 hours. What was the positive difference between the average speeds of both trips, in mph?

3. If a is not zero and $a = \frac{4}{5}b$, compute $\frac{12a+8b}{11a}$.

4. Compute the largest four-digit integer that is divisible by 11 such that all digits are prime and not all digits are the same.

5. For how many integer values of n is $n^2 - 10n + 16$ negative?

6. Steve is writing the Target Round and is trying to put the 8 questions he has chosen in order. It doesn't matter if he switches around questions 1 and 2 (since these are paired together anyway), or 3 and 4, or 5 and 6, or 7 and 8, but it does matter which order the pairs come in. How many different Target Rounds can Steve write?

7. In triangle ABC, let X, Y, and Z be the midpoints of $\overline{AB}$, $\overline{BC}$, and $\overline{CA}$ respectively. Given that the area of triangle ABC is 84, compute the area of triangle XYZ.

8. Compute the remainder when 20^{15} is divided by 18.

9. How many ways are there to fill a 3×3 grid with 0s, 1s, and 2s such that no two numbers in the same row are the same and no two numbers in the same column are the same?

10. Define point I in triangle ABC to be the center of the triangles inscribed circle. If $\angle BAC = 54°$, compute the measure, in degrees, of $\angle BIC$.

1. If the ratio of the area of square A to the area of square B is $\frac{91}{42}$, what is the ratio of the side length of square A to the side length of square B? Express your answer as a common fraction in simplest radical form.

2. Points A and B have the same y-coordinate of 8 but different x-coordinates. What is the sum of the y-intercept and slope of line AB?

3. How many positive integer factors does 6006 have?

4. Henry wants to get at least 70% on a test with 45 problems. What is the least number of problems Henry must get right on the test to achieve his goal?

5. Compute: $1 + 2 + 3 + \cdots + 15$.

6. How many positive perfect cube factors does $2^2 \cdot 3^3 \cdot 4^4 \cdot 5^5$ have?

7. The third and seventh term of a geometric sequence are 4 and 8, respectively. What is the fifteenth term of the sequence?

8. The sum of four consecutive odd integers is 272. What is the smallest of the four integers?

9. A circle has a radius of 34 cm and a chord of the circle is 32 cm long. How many centimeters is the midpoint of the chord from the center of the circle?

10. For what value of y does the equation $5x - 2x - 3 + 6 = 3x + y - 1$ have infinitely many solutions for x?

11. Suppose that x is a positive integer such that x has a remainder of 2 when divided by 5, a remainder of 3 when divided by 6, and a remainder of 6 when divided by 9. What is the least possible value of x?

12. Compute: $\sqrt{4096} - \sqrt{\sqrt{\sqrt{4096}}}$.

13. The number 36! ends with how many zeroes?

14. If a square has one side with a length of $7x - 23$ and another side with a length of $3x + 9$, what is the area of the square?

15. Maggie has three candles, which will burn for 4, 7, and 9 hours. If she wants to keep two candles burning at all times, what is the greatest number of hours she can burn the candles?

16. Find the sum of all primes less than 20.

17. If the first and second term of a geometric sequence are $\frac{1}{4}$ and $\frac{1}{3}$, what is the fourth term of the geometric sequence? Express your answer as a common fraction.

18. Robert burns 110 calories for every mile he runs. If he runs 2 miles a day for a week, how many calories did he burn while running during the week?

19. Find the sum of the first thirteen terms of the arithmetic sequence $9, 14, 19, \ldots$.

20. How many triangular numbers are two-digit numbers?

21. Susan borrowed $\$15,000$, and she had to pay back 140% of what she borrowed. How many dollars did she pay back?

22. How many square numbers less than 500 are divisible by 12?

23. Compute: $(\frac{1}{3} + \frac{1}{4})(\frac{1}{3} - \frac{1}{4})$. Express your answer as a common fraction.

24. What is the maximum number of 27 cent stamps that can be purchased with $\$20$?

25. Compute: $98 \cdot 98$.

26. If point A is at $(-5, -8)$ and point B is at $(11, 12)$, what is the x-coordinate of the x-intercept of the perpendicular bisector of segment AB? Express your answer as a common fraction.

27. Find the number of degrees in the measure of the supplement of the complement of an angle with a measure of 31 degrees.

28. What is the positive difference between 27% of 500 and 25% of 700?

29. What is the 20th term in the arithmetic sequence $\frac{4}{5}, \frac{6}{5}, \frac{8}{5}, \ldots$? Express your answer as a common fraction.

30. Daniel randomly picks 4 balls without replacement from a box with 5 yellow balls and 7 green balls. What is the probability that he picked 3 yellow balls and 1 green ball? Express your answer as a common fraction.

31. Compute: $\frac{49987}{7} + \frac{90013}{7}$.

32. A tree grew from a height of 16 feet to 36 feet. By what percent did its height increase?

33. The product of two integers with a difference of 4 is 957. What is the sum of the two integers?

34. If $x = 6$ and $y = 14$, find the value of $\frac{x+y}{\frac{1}{x}+\frac{1}{y}}$.

35. Leo drove to work from home at an average rate of 75 mph and returned home from work at an average rate of 50 mph. How many miles per hour was his average speed from both trips?

36. If the interior diagonal of a cube has a length of 7 cm, what is the surface area of the cube, in cm^2?

37. Mark and Frank each selected a positive integer less than 200. Mark's number is a multiple of 14 and Frank's number is a multiple of 35. What is the probability that they chose the same number? Express your answer as a common fraction.

38. How many diagonals does a regular dodecagon have?

39. The product of three consecutive integers is 124950. What is the sum of the three numbers?

40. Two concentric circles have radii of 22 cm and 28 cm. What is the area of the region in the larger circle outside of the smaller circle? Express your answer in terms of π.

41. What is the sum of all integer values of x such that $\frac{4}{x}$ is greater than $\frac{1}{5}$ and less than 2?

42. What is the sum of all the numbers in the top 6 rows of Pascal's triangle? The top row is the row with only one 1.

43. What is the surface area of a cylinder with a base radius of 5 cm and a height of 10 cm, in cm^2? Express your answer in terms of π.

44. A rectangular box has a length of 6 inches, a width of 8 inches, and a height of 9 inches. What is the length of the interior diagonal of the box? Express your answer in simplest radical form.

45. Donald borrows $4000 with simple interest at a rate of 5% per year. What is the total amount of interest, in dollars, that Donald needs to pay after 5 years?

46. Compute: $\text{LCM}(12, 24, 18) + \text{GCD}(12, 24, 18)$.

47. If the surface area of a sphere is π cm^2, what is the volume of the sphere, in cm^3? Express your answer as a common fraction in terms of π.

48. What is the arithmetic mean of 63, 67, 71, 75, 79, and 83?

49. What is the largest four-digit number that is divisible by 13?

50. How many ways are there to arrange 2 identical math books, 3 identical English books, and 2 identical history books on a shelf?

51. Two standard 6-sided dice are rolled. What is the probability that the positive difference between the values on both dice is a prime number? Express your answer as a common fraction.

52. At a toy factory, each worker assembles one toy at a time and can assemble a total of 28 toys in 2 hours. At this rate, how many toys can 9 workers assemble in 5 hours?

53. Compute the value of $(8x^3 - 20x^2 + 4x + 3)(2x - 5)$ when $x = 2.5$.

54. A number is increased by 40% and then the result is decreased by 40%. What is the percent of decrease from the original number to the final number?

55. What is the value of x for which $(x + 11)^2 = x^2$? Express your answer as a common fraction.

56. When a number is divided by 12, the quotient is 11 and the remainder is 10. What is the number?

57. The points $(1, 5), (4, 6), (3, 9)$, and $(0, 8)$ are the midpoints of the sides of a square. What is the area of the square?

58. If 1 skip equals 4 hops and 2 jumps equal 3 skips, how many hops are in a hop, skip, and a jump?

59. Loreen had a bag of candy. She gave $\frac{1}{2}$ of her candy to Wendy, $\frac{1}{4}$ of her remaining candy to Kathryn, and her last 12 pieces of candy to Cindy. How many pieces of candy did Wendy get?

60. If $x = 4$, find the value of $-2x^2 + 7x - 3$.

61. Rectangle $ABCD$ has side $AB = 12$ and side $BC = 7$. If E, F, and G are the midpoints of AB, BC, and CD, respectively, what is the area of triangle EFG?

62. A triangle has two sides of length 23 cm and 29 cm. What is the number of centimeters in the positive difference between the greatest and least possible whole number length of the third side?

63. The sum of two numbers is 3 and the difference between the squares of the two numbers is 57. What is the sum of the squares of the two numbers?

64. A worker earns $11 per hour for the first 45 hours worked in a week and 25% more than this amount per hour for any work over 45 hours. If the worker earned $825 in a week, how many hours did the worker work?

65. If $f(x) = 3x^2 - 5x - 7$ and $g(x) = x^3 - 27$, what is the value of $g(f(3))$?

66. For any number x, $x@ = x - 11$ and $@x = 8 - x$. What is the value of $@(20@)$?

67. How many square inches are in the area of a circle inscribed in a regular hexagon with sides of length 4 inches? Express your answer in terms of π.

68. There are chicken and horses in a barn. If there are 777 heads and 2222 legs in the barn, how many horses are in the barn?

69. The average of the numbers 29 and x is 14. What is the positive difference between 29 and x?

70. Two concentric circles have radii of 20 cm and 29 cm. What is the length of a chord of the larger circle tangent to the smaller circle, in cm?

71. Find the sum of the five smallest positive square numbers.

72. The mean of ten test scores is 88. When the lowest score is dropped, the mean of the remaining nine scores is 90. What is the value of the score which was dropped?

73. Express the ratio of 0.54 to 16.2 as a common fraction.

74. Find the sum of the squares of all solutions of $x^2 - 7x + 5 = 0$.

75. What is the least integer greater than 2015 that is divisible by 15?

76. Solve for x: $\frac{2-x}{2x-1} + \frac{x-2}{2-x} = -12$. Express your answer as a common fraction.

77. The length of a rectangle is decreased by 4 inches to create a square that has an area of 121 square inches. What is the perimeter of the rectangle, in inches?

78. The radius of a circle is 5 inches. When the radius is tripled, by how many square inches is the area increased? Express your answer in terms of π.

79. Compute: $\frac{\sqrt{169-144}}{\sqrt{169}-\sqrt{144}}$.

80. If m and n are integers, $24 < m < 55$ and $44 < n < 75$, what is the greatest possible value of $\frac{m+n}{n}$? Express your answer as a common fraction.

Sprint Test

1. 210
2. 58
3. 0
4. 24
5. 10001
6. $\frac{1}{3}$
7. 800
8. $\frac{13}{21}$
9. 100
10. $\frac{95}{3}$ (km)
11. 1
12. 3
13. 1
14. $72 + 72\sqrt{2}$
15. 53
16. $108\sqrt{3}$
17. 0
18. 45
19. 7
20. $\frac{11}{2}$
21. 395
22. 0
23. 72
24. 5
25. 5
26. 256
27. 0
28. 32
29. 6
30. $\frac{1}{2}$

Target Test

1. 12
2. 25
3. 380
4. 4056
5. 5
6. 15
7. 60
8. 9

Team Test

1. 30 (m)
2. 5 (mph)
3. 2
4. 7755
5. 5
6. 2520
7. 21
8. 8
9. 12
10. 117

Countdown

1. $\frac{\sqrt{78}}{6}$

2. 8

3. 32

4. 32

5. 120

6. 16

7. 32

8. 65

9. 30 (cm)

10. 4

11. 87

12. 56

13. 8

14. 1089

15. 10 (hours)

16. 77

17. $\frac{16}{27}$

18. 1540 (calories)

19. 507

20. 10

21. ($) 21000

22. 3

23. $\frac{7}{144}$

24. 74

25. 9604

26. $\frac{11}{2}$

27. 121 (degrees)

28. 40

29. $\frac{42}{5}$

30. $\frac{14}{99}$

31. 20000

32. 125(%)

33. 62

34. 84

35. 60 (mph)

36. 98 (cm^2)

37. $\frac{1}{35}$

38. 54

39. 150

40. 300π

41. 187

42. 63

43. 150π (cm^2)

44. $\sqrt{181}$

45. ($)1000

46. 78

47. $\frac{\pi}{6}$ (cm^3)

48. 73

49. 9997

50. 210

51. $\frac{4}{9}$

52. 630 (toys)

53. 0

54. 16(%)

55. $-\frac{11}{2}$

56. 142

57. 20

58. 11

59. 16 (pieces of candy)

60. -7

61. 21

62. 44 (cm)

63. 185

64. 69 (hours)

65. 98

66. -1

67. 12π

68. 334

69. 30

70. 42 (cm)

71. 55

72. 70

73. $\frac{1}{30}$

74. 39

75. 2025

76. $\frac{3}{7}$

77. 52 (inches)

78. 200π

79. 5

80. $\frac{11}{5}$

Sprint Test Solutions

1. Be sure to simplify before doing any calculations. The denominator will cancel out the 8 in the numerator and turn the 9 into a 3, so we just have to multiply 10, 3, and 7.

2. This is $2 \cdot 2 + 3(2 \cdot 3 + 3 \cdot 4) = 58$.

3. Note that the areas are the same because the two triangles have the same height and the base of each is half the base of ABC. So the difference is 0.

4. All three hexagons meet at a single vertex, and each hexagon has two edges that adjoin another hexagon, leaving four exposed edges per hexagon. This gives us a total of 12 exposed edges, each of length 2.

5. Note that $20152015 = 2015 \cdot 10001$, so the answer is either 10000 or 10001. However, clearly, 10000 is not a factor of 20152015, so the answer is 10001.

6. This is $\frac{15-12}{9} = \frac{1}{3}$.

7. If a side is x, the two areas are x^2 and $(3x)^2$, an increase of $8x$ which is 800% of x.

8. This is $\frac{\frac{2}{7}}{\frac{6}{13}} = \frac{13}{21}$.

9. There are five choices for the first digit (zero is not allowed), 5 for the second digit, and 4 for the third digit. $5 \times 5 \times 4 = 100$

10. In three days, Jonathan must complete $\frac{5}{11}$ of the 209 km, or 95 km.

11. $x^2 + 4 \le 4x \rightarrow (x-2)^2 \le 0$
    This inequality is only true when $x = 2$.

12. Use the formula for the sum of a geometric series: $\frac{a}{1-r}$, where a is the first term and r is the ratio between terms. The first term is $\frac{3}{5}$ and the ratio is $\frac{4}{5}$, so the sum is 3.

13. Note that $x^4, x^8 \ge 0$, so $1 + x^4 + x^8 \ge 1$. Setting $x = 0$ shows that this is achievable, so we are done.

14. There is a formula for this, but there's no need to memorize such things. Rest the octagon on an edge and then draw the two vertical diagonals and the two horizontal diagonals. We have nine regions now: a center square with side length 6, four isosceles right triangles with hypotenuse 6, and four 6 by $3\sqrt{2}$ rectangles (do you see why?). The square's area is 36, each triangle's area is 9, and each rectangle's area is $18\sqrt{2}$. $36 + 4 \cdot 9 + 4 \cdot 18\sqrt{2} = 72 + 72\sqrt{2}$.

15. Let the roots be p and q. We know that $p + q = -9$ and $pq = 14$, so $p^2 + q^2 = (p+q)^2 - 2pq = 81 - 28 = 53$. Feel free to use the quadratic formula instead if you want, but it's a trap!

16. The largest triangle will be equilateral. If this is not immediately apparent, consider any triangle inscribed in the circle. If it is not already equilateral, the area can be increased by finding a vertex that is not as far as possible from the opposite side and moving it to the point on the circle that is as far as possible from the opposite side. Continuing this process indefinitely will yield triangles that are closer and closer to equilateral. Anyway, if the radius is 12, the height of the triangle is 18 and the base is $12\sqrt{3}$, giving us an area of $108\sqrt{3}$.

17. First notice that $\sqrt{x-1} \ge 0 \rightarrow 2 + \sqrt{x-1} \ge 2$. Therefore the left hand side of this equation is no smaller than two. On the other hnd $x - 1 \ge 0 \rightarrow -x \le -1$ which means that the right hand side of the equation is no larger than -1. The intersection of these two intervals is empty, so this equation doesn't have any real solutions.

18. This is only true for the integers: $1 + 2 + 3 + 4 + 5 + 6 + 7 + 8 + 9 = 45$.

19. Factor out an x^2 from the first two terms and a -49 from the last two terms: $x^2(x+1) - 49(x+1)$. Now the $x + 1$ factors from both terms to give us $(x+1)(x^2 - 49) = (x+1)(x+7)(x-7)$ and the largest root is 7.

20. Extend the side with vertices $(3, 4)$ and $(0, 1)$

to $(-1, 0)$. This forms a triangle with base 3, height 4, and area 6 by adding a triangle of area $\frac{1}{2}$, so the area of the quadlilateral is $\frac{11}{2}$. Gauss's area formula (a.k.a. the Shoelace Formula) is great to know for such problems, and works particularly well here as 6 of 8 terms are 0. Look it up! While you're at it, Pick's Theorem is a great way to solve this one as well since the vertices are all lattice points.

21. Note that, if the answer is an integer, its units digit must be 5. Note that $m^3 \approx 62 \times 10^6$, so the root is slightly less than 400. Try 395 and it works.

22. Note that this product is the same as $2.015 \times 10^1 \times 5.102 \times 10^{-4} = p \times 10^{-3}$, where p is slightly larger than 10. Hence, this product is slightly larger than 1.0×10^{-2}. Hence, $a + b$ is slightly great than -1. So our answer is 0.

23. The area of the square is 36, and the combined area of the equilateral triangles is $4\left(\frac{6^2\sqrt{3}}{4}\right) = 36\sqrt{3}$, so the area is $36 + 36\sqrt{3}$ and our answer is 72.

24. Let the sum be S. Using the formula for the sum of the first n squares gives $S = \frac{(2014)(2015)(4029)}{6} = (1007)(2015)(1343) \equiv 7 \cdot 5 \cdot 3 \equiv 5 \pmod{10}$. Alternatively, we can find the sum of the first ten squares modulo 10, multiply that quantity by 201 and add the sum of the first four squares modulo 10.

25. Let r be the radius of ω, let O be its center, let M_1 be the midpoint of $\overline{AB}$, and let M_2 be the midpoint of $\overline{CD}$. We have that $AO = BO = M_2 O = r$ (by symmetry). Since

Target Test Solutions

1. Notice that a number is multiple of 5 if the unit of the number is 5 or 0, also notice that repetition of digits is NOT allowed. Therefore $2 \times 3 \times 2 \times 1 \times 1 = 12$.

2. An isosceles right triangle has side ratios of $1 : 1 : \sqrt{2}$. If the hypoteneuse is 10, the sides

$M_1 M_2 = 8$, $M_1 O = 8 - r$. Also $AM_1 = 4$. By the Pythagorean Theorem on triangle $AM_1 O$, we have $4^2 + (8 - r)^2 = r^2$, and solving yields $r = 5$.

26. $(1 + i)^2 = 2i$, and $(2i)^2 = -4$. Thus $(1 + i)^{16} = (2i)^8 = (-4)^4 = 256$. Alternately, using De Moivre's Theorem, we could write $z = 1 + i = \sqrt{2}e^{\frac{i\pi}{4}}$, and $z^{16} = 2^8 \cdot e^{4i\pi} = 256$.

27. Note that the remainder when N is divided by 9 is the same as the remainder when the sum of the digits of N is divided by 9. Because of this, adding the digits of all the integers from 1 to 2015 gives us the same remainder as when we add the integers from 1 to 2015. This sum is $\frac{2015 \cdot 2016}{2} = 2031120$. Adding the digits of this number, we find that the answer is 0.

28. By basic exponent rules, $\left(\sqrt{4}^{\sqrt{125}}\right)^{\sqrt{5}} = 2^{\sqrt{625}} = 2^{25}$. Then $\sqrt[5]{2^{25}} = 2^5 = 32$.

29. Case 1: $x, x^2, 2x^3$ in that order. Then, $x = 2x$, so $x = 0$. Case 2: $x, 2x^3, x^2$ in that order. Then, $2x^2 = \frac{1}{2x} \implies 4x^3 = 1 \implies x^3 = \frac{1}{4}$. Case 3: $x^2, x, 2x^3$ in that order. Then, $\frac{1}{x} = 2x^2 \implies 2x^3 = 1 \implies x^3 = \frac{1}{2}$. Hence, the answer is $\frac{1}{\sqrt[3]{2}} + \frac{1}{\sqrt[3]{4}} = 2^{-1/3} + 2^{-2/3}$, so $4S = 2^{5/3} + 2^{4/3}$, and our answer is $\lceil 4S \rceil = 6$.

30. Let $x = 18°, y = 27°$. Then the middle term is $\frac{1}{2}\sin 2x \sin 2y = 2 \sin x \sin y \cos x \cos y$. Thus our expression becomes $\sin^2 x \cos^2 y + 2 \sin x \sin y \cos x \cos y + \sin^2 y \cos^2 x$, which equals $(\sin x \cos y + \sin y \cos x)^2 = \sin^2(x + y)$, so our answer is $\sin^2 45° = \frac{1}{2}$.

must each be $\frac{10}{\sqrt{2}}$. The area of the triangle must be $\frac{1}{2} \cdot \left(\frac{10}{\sqrt{2}}\right)^2 = \frac{1}{2} \cdot \frac{100}{2} = 25$. Thus the area of the triangle must be 25.

3. The border of the patio will be 11 by 13, so the pool plus the patio has area of $143 - 48 = 95$ square meters. At 4 stones per square meter, Mr. DJ will need 380 of them.

4. Because 2027 and 2029 are both prime, the answer is $2027 + 2029 = 4056$.

5. This is $\frac{x}{y} = 5$.

6. Give two candies to Jeff immediately. Then we are looking for the number of ways to distribute the remaining four candies among the three people. By the "Stars and Bars" method, or by brute force, there are $\binom{6}{4} = 15$ ways to do

this.

7. There are 5 choices for the first letter, 4 for the second, and 3 for the third.

8. Note by rationalizing a fraction in the form $\frac{1}{\sqrt{n}+\sqrt{n+1}}$, we get $\frac{1}{\sqrt{n}+\sqrt{n+1}} \cdot \frac{\sqrt{n+1}-\sqrt{n}}{\sqrt{n+1}-\sqrt{n}} = \frac{\sqrt{n+1}-\sqrt{n}}{(\sqrt{n+1})^2-(\sqrt{n})^2} = \sqrt{n+1} - \sqrt{n}$. Thus all but two of the terms cancel in the desired sum, and it telescopes to $\sqrt{100} - \sqrt{1} = 9$.

Team Test Solutions

1. The square has side length of 5, so the yard is 7 by 8 so those are the 2 long sides of the desired area. It is 2 wide on one side of the garden, and 3 on the other. We also have to add in the two 5 meter borders with the garden for a total of $7+8+2+3+10 = 30$. Of course we could have saved a little time by just finding the perimeter of the whole yard (do you see why)?

2. Brian's first trip took 6 hours, and his second trip took 5 hours. His speed for the first trip was $\frac{150}{6} = 25$ mph, and his speed for the second trip was $\frac{150}{5} = 30$ mph, for a difference of 5 mph.

3. We have $\frac{5}{4}a = b$, so $\frac{12a+8b}{11a} = \frac{22a}{11a} = 2$.

4. Note that, to maximize our integer, we must first try to maximize its first digit; i.e. make it 7. Then, say the second digit was also 7. Then, let the last two digits be y and z in that order. The divisibility rule of 11 demands that $7 - 7 + y - z$ be divisible by 11. In other words, $y - z$ must be divisible by 11, so $y - z = 0$, implying $y = z$. If $y = z = 7$, all the digits are the same. Setting $y = z = 5$ works, so we are done.

5. The solutions to $n^2 - 10n + 16 = 0$ are $n = 2$, $n = 8$, so $n^2 - 10n + 16 < 0 \rightarrow 2 < n < 8$

Therefore there are five negative terms in this sequence.

6. There are $\binom{8}{2} = 28$ ways to select questions 1 and 2, $\binom{6}{2} = 15$ ways to select questions 3 and 4, $\binom{4}{2} = 6$ ways to select questions 5 and 6, and then 1 way to select questions 7 and 8. The total number of possible Target Rounds is $28 \cdot 15 \cdot 6 = 2520$.

7. By similarity, $[AXZ] = [BYX] = [CYZ] = \left(\frac{1}{2}\right)^2 \cdot 84 = 21$, so $[XYZ] = 84 - 3 \cdot 21 = 21$.

8. Since 20 has a remainder of 2 when divided by 18, this problem is equivalent to finding the remainder when 2^{15} is divided by 18. Because $2^5 = 32$ has a remainder of 14, we need to find the remainder when 14^3 is divided by 18, which is 8.

9. There are 6 ways to arrange 0, 1, and 2 in the first row. Then there will be 2 choices for each of these arrangements for the first cell of the second row after which the rest of the cells are determined.

10. Let $A = \angle BAC$, $B = \angle ABC$, and $C = \angle ACB$. Since I is the intersection of the angle bisectors of $\triangle ABC$, we have that $\angle CBI = \frac{B}{2}$ and $\angle BCI = \frac{C}{2}$. Then, $\angle BIC = 180 - \frac{B}{2} - \frac{C}{2} = 90 + \left(90 - \frac{B}{2} - \frac{C}{2}\right) = 90 + \frac{A}{2} = 117°$.

Sprint Test
Round 11515

Name: _____

Grade: _____

School: _____

place ID sticker inside this box

Score: #1 _____ Scorer's Initials _____

Score: #2 _____ Scorer's Initials _____

1.	2.	3.	4.	5.
6.	7.	8.	9.	10.
11.	12.	13.	14.	15.
16.	17.	18.	19.	20.
21.	22.	23.	24.	25.
26.	27.	28.	29.	30.

1. If $a\clubsuit b = 2a - 3b + 2ab$, what is the value of $3\clubsuit 4$?

2. What percent of 1.6 is 1.2?

3. What number is halfway between -7.2 and 12.8?

4. The difference between two natural numbers is 3 and the product is 40. What is the sum of the two numbers?

5. Mrs. Curtis conducted a survey regarding her students' pets. Five students had at least one dog, nine had at least one cat, three students had both dogs and cats, and seven had no dogs or cats. How many students were surveyed?

6. If x is one-third of 10, what is three-fourths of $8x$?

7. The sum of 5 consecutive integers is $5x$, and the largest of the five integers is N. What is $N - x$?

8. Sally is removing marbles from a bag. There are 5 white marbles, 6 red marbles, and 7 blue marbles. Find the minimum number of marbles Sally can remove that guarantees she will have three marbles of the same color.

9. A fresh potion of invisibility costs 18000 copper pieces. Once it passes its "sell by" date, the Witch of Doom discounts the potion 15% After it passes its expiration date, she discounts it an additional 40%. Adam, who receives a meager allowance, is hunting for a bargain, so he selects the double-discounted potion. What percentage of the original price does he pay?

10. In a movie theater, the first row has 10 chairs, the second 12, the third 14, and so on. If the theater has 24 rows, how many seats are there?

11. The number $0.\overline{2} + 0.\overline{013}$ expressed as a fraction in lowest terms is $\frac{a}{b}$. Find $a + b$.

12. If A, B, C, D are four distinct integers between 0 to 9 inclusive, what is the largest possible integer value of $\frac{A+C}{B+C} + D$?

13. Two fair six-sided dice are rolled. What is the probability that the sum shown is divisible by 4? Express your answer as a common fraction.

14. How many two digit numbers that are divisible by 3 have one or more digits that is a 3?

15. The base of a triangle is one-third its height, and the area of the triangle is 216. How long is the base of the triangle?

16. What are the coordinates of the point which is 40% of the way from the point $(-10, 25)$ to the point $(25, -10)$? Express your answer as an ordered pair.

17. A potion from the Witch of Doom is 100% effective on the day it expires, and thereafter, its effectiveness decreases according to the function $y = -3x + 100$, where x is the number of days since the expiration date, and y is the percentage of the potion's original effectiveness. If Adam purchases the potion 28 days after it expires, how effective will the potion be that day? Express your answer as a percentage.

18. A right triangle on the two-dimensional plane with one vertex on each axis and one at the origin is isosceles and has area 200. Let the length of the longest side of the triangle be ℓ. Compute ℓ^4.

19. Calvin runs for 2 miles at an average speed of 5 miles per hour. He stops for 10 minutes to rest. He finishes up by running for half an hour at 4.5 miles per hour. What is his average speed in miles per hour for the entire workout? Round your answer to two decimal places.

20. A man traveled 87 miles north. Then, he drove east for 116 miles. Now, how far in miles is the man from his starting point?

21. Find the sum of all values of x for which $\sqrt{2 + x} = x$.

22. Gary rolls a 20-sided die twice. What is the probability of him rolling an odd number, then an even number? Express your answer as a common fraction.

23. What is the units digit of 7^{29}?

24. When the positive integers a, b, and c are divided by 13, the respective remainders are 9, 7, and 10. What is the remainder when $a + 8b - 9c$ is divided by 13?

25. Let n be the rational number with $\frac{n}{n + \frac{1}{1 + \frac{1}{15}}} = \frac{1}{20}$. If $n = \frac{a}{b}$ in lowest terms (with a and b integers), find $a + b$.

26. Compute the remainder when 2014! is divided by 2015.

27. In a geometric sequence, the first term is 7, and the common ratio is 2. If the nth term is 224, what is n?

28. Solve for n, if $\frac{n}{14} + 12 = 87$.

29. Compute the sum of the digits of $1234567890 \cdot 1234567891 - 1234567890^2$.

30. What is the value of $\log_{\frac{1}{9}} 3\sqrt{3}$? Express your answer as a common fraction.

Target Test
Round 11515

Name: _____

Grade: _____

School: _____

place ID sticker inside this box

Score: #1 _____ Scorer's Initials _____

Score: #2 _____ Scorer's Initials _____

1. What is the sum of all of the 2-digit odd positive integers?

1.

2. What is the acute angle formed by the hands of a standard analog clock at 8 : 20, in degrees?

2.

Name: _____

Grade: _____

School: _____

place ID sticker inside this box

Score: #3 _____ Scorer's Initials _____

Score: #4 _____ Scorer's Initials _____

3. Mr. Nimoy just finished paying for a rent-to-own mechanical rice picker. If he paid a total of 30% more than the sticker price of $720 in 24 equal monthly payments, what was each monthly payment in dollars?

3.

4. What is the smallest positive integer that leaves a remainder of 7 when divided by 8, 8 when divided by 9, and 9 when divided by 10?

4.

Name: _____

Grade: _____

School: _____

place ID sticker inside this box

Score: #5 _____   Scorer's Initials _____

Score: #6 _____   Scorer's Initials _____

5. For how many integer values of x is $(x + 20)(x + 15) \leq 0$?

5.

6. What is the volume of a regular tetrahedron of side length 12?

6.

Name: _____

Grade: _____

School: _____

place ID sticker inside this box

Score: #7 _____ Scorer's Initials _____

Score: #8 _____ Scorer's Initials _____

7. A hoopy number is a positive integer containing the digit 4 immediately followed by the digit 2. How many hoopy numbers are less than 10000?

7.

8. In a geometric sequence with positive terms, each term is the sum of the two previous terms of the sequence. What is the value of the common ratio of the sequence? Express your answer as a decimal to the nearest hundredth.

8.

Team Test
Round 11515

School/ Team:

Score: #1 _____ Scorer's Initials _____

Score: #2 _____ Scorer's Initials _____

name or ID sticker goes in this box

name or ID sticker goes in this box

name or ID sticker goes in this box

name or ID sticker goes in this box

name or ID sticker goes in this box

name or ID sticker goes in this box

1.

2.

3.

4.

5.

6.

7.

8.

9.

10.

1. Dayal had 3 coupons, each good to be used for one item at his favorite model polyhedron store. If the coupons were for 40%, 25%, and 10% off, and the three items he bought had regular prices of 50 euros, 40 euros, and 20 euros, what is the least number of euros he could have spent?

2. How many multiples of 7 are there between 100 and 500?

3. How many different triangles have all integer side lengths and a perimeter of 9? Two triangles are the same if the sides are the same in any order.

4. After a routine adventure, Bronwyn discovers a pair of magical seven-league boots in a pile of treasure. When she wears them, each step she takes carries her 7 leagues. (A league is 3 miles.) When she takes them off, she walks normally. No small, partial, or special steps are allowed. She wants to visit her fairy grandmother who lives 185 miles away. What is the fewest number of miles she can walk in regular shoes to get to her destination?

5. A *plonker* is a positive integer whose digits are all 6s and 0s. Compute the remainder when the 11th smallest plonker is divided by 11.

6. Every gameday, 23 athletes stand in a circle, and every athlete shakes hands with the athlete immediately to his left and right. The lineup order is not the same every day, but the set of athletes is. What is the minimum number of gamedays it could take for every pair of athletes to shake hands at least once?

7. In an arithmetic sequence, the mth term is $2n$, and the nth term $2m$, for some values of m and n. What is the common difference of this sequence? Express your answer as an integer.

8. The surface area of a cube is 294 square units. Find the cube's volume.

9. A band tightly bundles seven pipes of diameter 10 meters such that the cross section along the plane of the band reveals a central circle tangent to and surrounded by 6 pairwise tangent circles (just as you would expect a tight bundle to be). The length of the band is $a + b\pi$ meters. Compute $a + b$.

10. Let the two real solutions to $x^2 - 9x + 4 = 0$ be r and s. If the solutions to $x^2 - ax + b = 0$ are r^3 and s^3, compute $1 - a + b$.

1. Farmer Steve has only cows and chickens on his farm. His farm animals have a total of 84 legs. What is the difference between the greatest and least number of animals he could have on his farm?

2. Compute: $81 + 135 + 225 + 375 + 625$.

3. Compute: $\frac{2.7}{2.5} + \frac{7.3}{2.5}$.

4. If Robby drove at 40 miles per hour for 48 minutes, how many miles did he travel?

5. What is the ratio of volume to surface area of a sphere with a radius of 4? If appropriate, express your answer as a common fraction.

6. Simplify: $\frac{3030}{202}$.

7. The sum of 4 consecutive integers is 46. What is the product of those integers?

8. What is the exponent of the 5 in the prime factorization of 50! ?

9. What is the probability, expressed as a common fraction, that exactly four heads will come up when seven fair coins are flipped?

10. Simplify: $\frac{8!-7!}{8!}$. Express your answer as a common fraction.

11. What is the sum of first 39 positive integers?

12. How many seconds does it take the hour hand on a clock to rotate 25 degrees?

13. Evaluate: 73×67.

14. What is the expected number of rolls it will take until a standard six-sided die first lands on a 6?

15. For what value of k is there no solution to the equations $8x + 3y = 24$ and $kx + 18y = 96$?

16. Find the perimeter, in units, of a rectangle with a length of 24 units and a diagonal of 25 units.

17. The arithmetic mean of 13 numbers is 54. What is their sum?

18. What is the least positive multiple of 68 that is also a square number?

19. How many positive integers less than 100 are divisible by 7?

20. Find the remainder when 5^{100} is divided by 100.

21. What is the greatest perfect square less than 10000?

22. The numbers $66, a, b, c, 20$ form an arithmetic sequence. What is the value of the sum $a + c$?

23. A baseball team lost 20% of the 90 games they played. How many games did they win?

24. Five people decide to have a gift sharing event and each of them makes a gift. The gifts are shuffled and randomly passed back, one to each person, such that no one receives their own gift. In how many ways can this happen?

25. If $a\spadesuit b = a^2 + 4ab + 4b^2$, what is $6\spadesuit(2\spadesuit 3)$?

26. A certain species of bacteria doubles in population every 48 hours. If a container starts off with one bacterium, after how many whole days would the total number of bacteria first exceed 1000?

27. Simplifiy: 121×32.

28. What is the area of the quadrilateral with vertices at $(1, 3)$, $(5, 7)$, $(2, 5)$, and $(6, 9)$? If appropriate, express your answer as a common fraction.

29. Evaluate: 23×23.

30. The sixth root of a number is 9. What is the square root of that number?

31. Compute: $\sqrt{3025}$.

32. What is the units digit of the product $408 \times 925 \times 916 \times 415$?

33. What is the product of all integers that are one less than a one-digit prime?

34. An 18-foot board is cut into two pieces whose lengths are in the ratio 1 to 5. What is the difference, in inches, between the lengths of the two pieces?

35. The perimeter of a regular pentagon is 65 cm. What is its side length in cm?

36. For integers a and b, what is the smallest possible positive value of $15a + 20b$?

37. What is the largest integer x for which $\frac{1}{x}$ is larger than $\frac{8}{49}$?

38. Set A has 9 elements and set B has 12 elements. The union of set A and B has 14 elements. How many elements are in the intersection of sets A and B?

39. The ratio of the measures of two complementary angles is 4:5. What is the difference between the measures of the two angles, in degrees?

40. Simplify: $\sqrt{676}$.

41. What is the sum of the coordinates of the midpoint of a line segment with its endpoints at (5, 8) and (13, 16)?

42. Henry flips a fair coin 6 times. What is the probability that he flips an odd number of heads? Express your answer as a common fraction.

43. If 2 adjacent sides of a parallelogram have lengths of 7 and 14 and the angle between them is 30 degrees, what is the area of the parallelogram?

44. If $x + y = 42$, $x + z = 18$, and $y + z = 56$, what is the value of $x + y + z$?

45. What is the product of the smallest prime number greater than 60 and the largest prime number less than 60?

46. How many pints are there in 5 gallons?

47. A random card is chosen from a regular deck of playing cards. What is the probability that it is a black face card (remember face cards are Jacks, Queens, and Kings)? Express your answer as a common fraction.

48. If $a + b = 10$ and $a^2 - b^2 = 60$, what is ab?

49. If a square with sides of length 12 is inscribed inside of an equilateral triangle, what is the side length of the triangle? Express your answer in simplest radical form.

50. The sum of 11 consecutive integers is 11. What is the largest of these integers?

51. Square ABCD has an area of 144. An octagon has all 8 of its vertices on the square, with 2 vertices on each side of the square, such that they trisect each side of the square. What is the area of the octagon?

52. Evaluate: 67×13.

53. The relationship between temperatures in Fahrenheit and Celsius is $F = \frac{9}{5}C + 32$, where F is the temperature in degrees Fahrenheit and C is the temperature in degrees Celsius. Convert 25 degrees Celsius to degrees Fahrenheit.

54. If there are 10 people at a meeting and each person shakes hands with every other person exactly once, how many handshakes are there?

55. If the length of a rectangle is 4 feet less than four times its width and its perimeter is 42 feet, what is the area of the rectangle?

56. What are the last two digits of 7^{2015}?

57. Evaluate: 31×22.

58. Express as a decimal: $6 \times 100 + 1 \times 1 + \frac{7}{10}$.

59. Kevin has 11 quarters, 8 dimes, 23 nickels, and 13 pennies. How many dollars does he have? Express your answer to the nearest hundredth.

60. What is the sum of the degree measures of the interior angles of a nonagon?

61. Compute: $345 + 678$.

62. An octagon is created by placing four equilateral triangles with sides of length 10 around a square with a side length of 10. What is the area of the octagon? Express your answer in simplest radical form.

63. Evaluate: $-1 + 2 + -3 + 4 + -5 + 6 \ldots + 20$.

64. What is the area of the region bounded by the x-axis, y-axis, and the line $2x + 5y = 20$?

65. If two positive integers have a sum of 29, what is their maximum possible difference?

66. If the average of 8 positive integers is 15, what is the maximum possible range of those integers?

67. A bag contains 6 red marbles, 2 blue marbles, and 4 purple marbles. One marble from the bag is randomly selected. What is the probability it is purple? Express your answer as a common fraction.

68. Simplify: 32×303.

69. N is an integer greater than 6, and when 198 is divided by N, the remainder is 6. For how many distinct positive integers N is this statement true?

70. A rectangular box has a volume of two quarts. If all of its dimensions are tripled, then what is the volume of the new box in quarts?

71. What is the least common multiple of the first six positive integers?

72. $x = 16$ and $y = 25$. What is $x\sqrt{y} + y\sqrt{x} + \sqrt{xy}$?

73. A quadrilateral has integer sides. Three of its sides have lengths of 9, 14, and 11. What is the positive difference between the maximum and minimum length of the fourth side?

74. What value of x satisfies $10! = 7! \cdot x$?

75. One leg of a right triangle is increased by 20% and the other leg is decreased by 15%. By what percent does the area of the triangle increase?

76. If Tom gives Andrew $8, they will have the same amount of money. If Andrew gives Tom $8, Tom will have twice as much money as Andrew. How many dollars do they have in total?

77. Given that $a^b = 25$ and a and b are both integers, what is the largest possible value of a?

78. There are eight teams in a football league. Each team plays each other team once. How many games are played in all?

79. If $5! = \frac{x!}{y!}$, what is the largest possible value of $x + y$?

80. If $|x - 18| = 5$, what are the sum of all possible values of x?

Sprint Test

1. 18
2. 75 (%)
3. 2.8
4. 13
5. 18
6. 20
7. 2
8. 7
9. 51 (%)
10. 792
11. 1234
12. 18
13. $\frac{1}{4}$
14. 6
15. 12
16. $(4, 11)$
17. 16 (%)
18. 640000
19. 3.98 (mph)
20. 145 (miles)
21. 2
22. $\frac{1}{4}$
23. 7
24. 1
25. 319

26. 0
27. 6
28. 1050
29. 45
30. $-\frac{3}{4}$

Target Test

1. 2475
2. 130 (degrees)
3. ($) 39
4. 359
5. 6
6. $144\sqrt{2}$
7. 299
8. 1.62

Team Test

1. 78
2. 57
3. 3
4. 4
5. 5
6. 11
7. -2
8. 343
9. 70
10. -556

Countdown

1. 21
2. 1441
3. 4
4. 32
5. $\frac{4}{3}$
6. 15
7. 17160
8. 12
9. $\frac{35}{128}$
10. $\frac{7}{8}$
11. 780
12. 3000
13. 4891
14. 6
15. 48
16. 62
17. 702
18. 1156
19. 14
20. 25
21. 9801
22. 86
23. 72
24. 44
25. 17956
26. 20

27. 3872
28. 4
29. 529
30. 729
31. 55
32. 0
33. 48
34. 144
35. 13
36. 5
37. 6
38. 7
39. 10
40. 26
41. 21
42. $\frac{1}{2}$
43. 49
44. 58
45. 3599
46. 40
47. $\frac{3}{26}$
48. 16
49. $8\sqrt{3} + 12$
50. 6
51. 112
52. 871
53. 77

54. 45
55. 80
56. 43
57. 682
58. 601.7
59. 4.83
60. 1260
61. 1023
62. $100 + 100\sqrt{3}$
63. 10
64. 20
65. 27
66. 112
67. $\frac{1}{3}$
68. 9696
69. 9
70. 54
71. 60
72. 200
73. 32
74. 720
75. 2(%)
76. 96
77. 25
78. 28
79. 9
80. 36

Sprint Test Solutions

1. This is $6 - 12 + 24 = 18$.

2. $\frac{1.2}{1.6} \times 100 = 75$

3. This is just the average of the 2 numbers.

4. The numbers are 8 and 5.

5. If there are 3 students who have a dog and a cat, then $5 - 3 = 2$ students have only dogs and $9 - 3 = 6$ have only cats. Thus the total number of students is $3 + 2 + 6 + 7 = 18$.

6. Three-fourths of $8x$ is $6x$, which is six-thirds of 10, or 20.

7. The average of the 5 is x, which is the middle integer, so the largest is $x + 2$, and $N - x = 2$.

8. There are 3 types of marbles in the bag. If Sally removes six marbles, she might not get three of the same color, but if not, she will have two of each color. If she removes a seventh marble, she will be guaranteed to have three of one color.

9. The first reduced price is $18000 - (18000 \cdot .15) = 15300$. The second reduced price is $15300 - (15300 \cdot .15) = 9180$. Since $9180 \div 18000 = .51$, Adam pays 51% of the original price.

10. The total number of seats is $10 + (10 + 2) + (10 + 4) + \cdots + (10 + 23 \cdot 2) = 24 \cdot 10 + 2 \cdot (1 + 2 + \cdots + 23)$. Using the formula for the sum of the first n integers, this is $240 + 23 \cdot 24 = 792$.

11. This is $\frac{2}{9} + \frac{13}{999} = \frac{222}{999} + \frac{13}{999} = \frac{235}{999}$.

12. We obviously want to make A and D as large as possible, and B as small as possible. Note that if $A > B$, then $\frac{A+C+1}{B+C+1} < \frac{A+C}{B+C}$, so we should also make C as small as possible. Thus A and D should be 8 and 9, and B and C should be 0 and 1. Given this, $B + C$ will always equal 1, so the expression is equal to $A + C + D$, and this is maximized when $C = 1$, $B = 0$, and $A + D = 8 + 9$. The maximum value is 18.

13. There are 36 possible rolls and 3 ways to roll a 4, 5 ways to roll an 8, and 1 way to roll a 12,

so the probability is $\frac{9}{36} = \frac{1}{4}$.

14. Since we know that one of the digits must be a 3, then the other digit must also be a multiple of 3 to make the number divisible by 3. That leaves us with 4 numbers for the other digit: 0, 3, 6, and 9. If the first digit is 3, we have 30, 33, 36, and 39. If the first digit is 6, we have 63. If the first digit is 9, we have 93. This gives us a total of 6.

15. Letting b be the length of the base, the height is $3b$, and the area is $\frac{3b^2}{2} = 216$. Solving gives $b = 12$.

16. When moving from $(-10, 25)$ to $(25, -10)$, the x-coordinate increases by 35, and the y-coordinate decreases by 35. 40% of 35 is 14, so to get 40% of the way there, we increase the x-coordinate by 14 and decrease the y-coordinate by 14, arriving at $(4, 11)$.

17. If $y = -3x + 100$, then 28 days after its expiration, the potion will be $-3(28) + 100 = 16\%$ effective. If Adam had purchased and drunk the potion on or before the expiration date, it would have conferred 60 minutes of 100% invisibility. If he had consumed it the day he bought it, he would have enjoyed 9.6 minutes of being 16% invisible, looking like a translucent ghost. Unfortunately, Adam waited 30 more days to drink the potion, and spent several hours as a hideous, vividly green monster. Apparently Adam was hoping to become invisible to avoid attention at school, but his plan backfired. Unfortunately, his transformation happened in the middle of history class. We can only hope that he is not doomed to repeat this mistake.

18. Let the edge length (non-hypotenuse) be x. Then, $200 = \frac{x^2}{2}$, giving $x^2 = 400$, so the answer is $\left(x\sqrt{2}\right)^2 = \left(2x^2\right)^2 = 800^2 = 640000$.

19. Calvin's average speed will equal the total distance he traveled divided by the total time it took. Break up his workout into different segments. Let d_1, d_2, and d_3 equal the dis-

tances Calvin ran during each segment and let t_1, t_2, and t_3 equal the time duration of each segment. First, he ran for 2 miles at 5 mph. $d_1 = 2$ miles and $t_1 = \frac{2}{5} = 0.4$ hours. Then, he rested for 10 minutes, so $d_2 = 0$ and $t_2 = \frac{10}{60} = 0.167$ hours (approximately). Finally, calculate the distance and time for the last stretch. $d_3 = 4.5 \cdot 0.5 = 2.25$ miles and $t_3 = 0.5$ hours. So, $d_{total} = 2 + 0 + 2.25 = 4.25$ miles and $t_{total} = 0.4 + 0.167 + 0.5 = 1.067$ hours (approximately). Calvin's average speed is approximately $\frac{4.25}{1.067} = 3.98$ mph.

20. The path the man traveled traces out a right triangle with legs of length 87 and 116. So, the net distance he traveled is the length of the hypotenuse. Notice that $87 = 3 \cdot 29$ and $116 = 4 \cdot 29$. The ratio of the shorter leg to the longer one is 3:4. For a right triangle with legs of length 3 and 4, the length of the hypotenuse is 5. ($3^2 + 4^2 = 5^2$) So, our large right triangle is simply a 3-4-5 right triangle scaled up by a factor of 29. Therefore, the net distance traveled is $5 \cdot 29$.

21. Square both sides of the equation. Then $x^2 - x - 2 = 0$; factoring, $(x-2)(x+1) = 0$, so $x = 2$ or $x = -1$. Standard convention is to assume a square root indicates the positive root unless stated otherwise, so the only solution is $x = 2$.

22. Since the die has an even number of faces, exactly half of the faces are even and the other half are odd. Thus, the probability of rolling an odd number first is $\frac{1}{2}$ and the probability of rolling an even number on the second roll is also $\frac{1}{2}$. The probability of both outcomes occurring is $\frac{1}{2} \cdot \frac{1}{2} = \frac{1}{4} = 0.25$

23. The units digits of powers of 7 cycle: 7,9,3,1,7,9,3,1,.... Since 29 is 1 more than a multiple of 4, the units digits of 7^{29} and 7^1 are the same.

24. Use a, b, and c's remainders instead of their actual values into $a + 8b - 9c$, to get -25. Then we take -25 mod 13 to arrive at 1.

25. First note that $\frac{1}{1 + \frac{1}{15}} = \frac{15}{16}$. Now cross-multiply to obtain $n + \frac{15}{16} = 20n$, so $n = \frac{15}{19 \cdot 16}$. Our answer is $15 + 19 \cdot 16 = 319$.

26. Since $2015 = 5 \cdot 13 \cdot 31$, and 2014! is divisible by 5, 13, and 31, 2014! is divisible by 2015, and the remainder is zero.

27. The sequence is 7, 14, 28, 56, 112, 224; the 6th term is 224.

28. $\frac{n}{14} = 87 - 12$, so $n = 75 \cdot 14 = 1050$.

29. Let $x = 1234567890$. Then, the answer is $x \cdot (x+1) - x^2 = x = 1234567890$. The sum of the digits is 45.

30. $\log_{\frac{1}{9}} 3\sqrt{3} = \log_{3^{-2}} 3^{\frac{3}{2}} = \frac{3}{2} \log_{3^{-2}} 3$. Since $\log_{3^{-2}} 3 = -\frac{1}{2}$, this is $-\frac{3}{4}$.

Target Test Solutions

1. The first is 11 and the last is 99, so the average of the numbers is $\frac{11 + 99}{2} = 55$, and there are 45 numbers, so the sum is $55 \cdot 45 = 2475$.

2. The angle between each number is $\frac{360°}{12} = 30°$. The minute hand is at the 4 mark and the hour hand is 1/3 of the way from the 8 mark to 9 mark. The angle between the 4 mark and the 8 mark is $4 \cdot 30° = 120°$. The angle between the 8 mark and the hour hand is $\frac{1}{3} \cdot 30° = 10°$. Hence, the angle between the hands is 130°.

3. Mr. Nimoy paid $720 \cdot 1.30 = \$936$ in total, and thus $\frac{1}{24} \cdot \$936 = \$39$ each month.

4. This number is one less than a multiple of 8, 9, and 10, so it is one less than a multiple of 360 (360 is the LCM of 8, 9, and 10). The smallest positive integer that is one less than a multiple of 360 is 359.

5. If $x + 20$ and $x + 15$ are either both positive or both negative, then the exression is positive. The only integer values for which this is not the case are $x = -15, -16, ..., -20$.

6. The volume is $\frac{1}{3}Bh$ where B is the area of the base and h is the height. The base is an equilateral triangle with side length 12, so it has area $36\sqrt{3}$. The height is measured from the center of the base, which is $4\sqrt{3}$ from a vertex (remember the distance from the vertex is $\frac{2}{3}$ of the altitude of the base). Set up an equation now using the Pythagorean Theorem: $h^2 + (4\sqrt{3})^2 = 12^2$, or $h^2 + 48 = 144$. This gives us $h = 4\sqrt{6}$ and we can plug into the original formula: $V = \frac{1}{3} \cdot 36\sqrt{3} \cdot 4\sqrt{6} = 144\sqrt{2}$.

7. If the 4 of 42 is the thousands digit, we have 100 choices for the last two digits. If the 4 is the hundreds digit, we have 10 choices each for the thousands and units digits (0 for the thousands digit counts all the 3-digit numbers) for 100 more. Similarly, there are 100 more with the 4 as the tens digit. We have double counted the super hoopy first order froodish number 4242 so there are 299 hoopy numbers less than 10000. Give yourself an award if you counted it this way, and make sure everyone hears about it.

8. Suppose the first term is 1, and the common ratio is r. Then the second term is r, and the third term is r^2. We must then have $1 + r = r^2$, or $r^2 - r - 1 = 0$. Using the quadratic formula, $r = \frac{1 \pm \sqrt{5}}{2}$. Since all the terms are positive, we want the positive value of r, which is $\frac{1+\sqrt{5}}{2} \approx 1.62$.

Team Test Solutions

1. To spend the least money, Dayal should use the best coupons on the most expensive items. The 50-euro item costs 30 euros at 40% off; the 40-euro item also costs 30 euros at 25% off, and the 20-euro item costs 18 euros at 19% off, for a total of $30 + 30 + 18 = 78$ euros.

2. Start by looking for the largest and smallest multiples in our range. The smallest multiple of 7 that is also greater than 100 is $7 \cdot 15 = 105$. The largest multiple less than 500 is $7 \cdot 71 = 497$. So, we want to count how many numbers are in the list $7 \cdot 15, 7 \cdot 16, \ldots, 7 \cdot 71$. Note that this is the same as asking how many integers are there between 15 and 71 inclusive. Add 1 to the difference between the bounds to get the answer. $71 - 15 + 1 = 57$.

3. The triangle inequality states that each side must be smaller than the sum of the other two sides. So the longest side can be no more than 4 and no less than 3. We have 4-4-1, 4-3-2, and 3-3-3 as the only possibilities.

4. At first, Bronwyn thinks she must take 8 steps to travel $8 \cdot 7 \cdot 3 = 168$ miles, then walk another 17 miles normally. Fortunately, she stops to think before lacing up the boots. She decides to take 9 steps, travel 189 miles, remove the magic boots, and then backtrack 4 miles in mundane footwear.

5. List 'em: 6, 60, 66, 600, 606, 660, 666, 6000, 6006, 6060, 6066. The remainder is 5.

6. Each athlete must shake hands with 22 others, so 11 gamedays will be required, at least. This can be achieved by numbering the athletes 1 through 23 (with 24 being the same as 1, 25 the same as 2, and so on). On the first day, athlete n stands next to $n + 1$ and $n - 1$. On the second day, n stands next to $n + 2$ and $n - 2$, and so on.

7. In general, if a_n and a_m are the nth and mth terms, the common difference is $\frac{a_n - a_m}{n - m}$. In this case, this is $\frac{2m - 2n}{n - m} = \frac{-2(n-m)}{n-m} = -2$.

8. A cube has 6 sides. All the sides are squares of side length x units. So, the surface area is equal to $6x^2$. Setting this expression equal to 294 and solving yields $x = 7$. The volume of a cube is simply x^3.

9. Looking at the cross-section, draw the line segments on the outside of the figure between each pair of tangent circles. Drawing radii from each circle to these tangent points and the tangent points with adjacent circles, we see that each of

these six segments is congruent to 2 radii, and so have a total length of 60. The band is also around an arc of each circle. Looking at the center of each circle, the lines thus far drawn form 2 right angles, and a third angle is an interior angle of a regular hexagon, $120°$. These leaves a $60°$ arc. 6 of these is a full circle with circumference of 10π giving a total band length of $60 + 10\pi$.

10. If the roots of $x^2 - 9x + 4$ are r and s, then the expression factors as $(x - r)(x - s) = x^2 - rx - sx + rs$, so $r + s = 9$ and $rs = 4$. Now, $(r+s)^3 = r^3 + 3r^2s + 3rs^2 + s^3 = r^3 + s^3 + 3rs(r + s)$. Substituting in, this gives $9^3 = r^3 + s^3 + 3 \cdot 4 \cdot 9$, so $r^3 + s^3 = 729 - 108 = 621$. Also, $r^3s^3 = (rs)^3 = 64$. By a similar argument, $a = r^3 + s^3$ and $b = r^3s^3$, so $1 - a + b = 1 - 621 + 64 = -556$.

Sprint Test
Round 11516

Name: _____

Grade: _____

School: _____

place ID sticker inside this box

Score: #1 _____ Scorer's Initials _____

Score: #2 _____ Scorer's Initials _____

1.	2.	3.	4.	5.
6.	7.	8.	9.	10.
11.	12.	13.	14.	15.
16.	17.	18.	19.	20.
21.	22.	23.	24.	25.
26.	27.	28.	29.	30.

1. A standard 8-by-8 chessboard is expanded to include one more row and one more column. How many unit squares must be added?

2. How many prime numbers are less than 110?

3. The product of three consecutive integers is greater than 8000. What is the smallest possible value of the middle integer?

4. What is the positive difference between the sum of the squares of the first 6 positive integers and the sum of the cubes of the first 6 positive integers?

5. Jack has 180 candies. He eats half of them, his brother eats two-thirds of the remaining candies, and then their twin sisters split the rest. how many candies did each sister get?

6. Joshua can compliment a Klingon musician every 5 minutes, while Aaron can compliment one every 6 minutes. It takes them exactly 14 days – minus 2 days off to take their pet Targ hunting – to compliment the entire population of Stovokor (made up entirely of musical Klingons) while complimenting for 8 hours a day. How many people dwell in Stovokor?

7. What is the area of the largest square that can be inscribed in a circle with area 9π?

8. A ball is dropped and bounces to a height of 1000 meters. Each time it hits the ground it bounces half as high as the bounce before. After how many total bounces will it remain within 1 meter of the ground?

9. Brian has 3 pet rectangles, Chewbacca, Saurav, and Chandan. Chewbacca is a square with an area of 16. Saurav's length is three times Chewbacca's whilst being half as wide. Chandan's width is twelve times Chewbacca's whilst being only one-quarter as long. How many times larger is Brian's largest pet than his smallest pet?

10. Find the greatest common divisor of 901 and 2014.

11. Janet has a cubic wooden block with sides 1 meter in length. She wishes to paint a border on each face 10 cm wide (every point within 10 cm of an edge will be painted). 100 milliliters of paint will cover 1 square meter. How many milliliters of paint will she need?

12. Evaluate $2^0 + 2^1 + 2^2 + \cdots + 2^{12}$.

13. The probability of drawing a red toy out of a chest is $\frac{1}{6}$. A child picks a toy out of the chest at random one day, plays with it, and puts it back. She does this three more times. What is the probability that she does not play with any red toys?

14. Express 121021_3 in base 7.

15. Bruno has coins with values of 1, 2, 5, and 10 Euros. If he has a total of 15 Euros, how many different combinations of coins could he have?

16. Find the sum of all the prime factors of the number 13035.

17. A kangaroo is hopping up a set of 12 stairs. It hops either 2 or 3 steps at a time. In how many ways can it hop up the stairs if it must land at the top exactly?

18. On a set of scales, a duck balances an eagle and an aardvark. An eagle balances an aardvark and a springbok. Two ducks balance three springboks. How many aardvarks balance an eagle?

19. Find the smallest positive x such that $\lfloor x \rfloor + \frac{1}{\lfloor 17x \rfloor} = x$. Express your answer as a decimal to the nearest hundredth. Note: $\lfloor x \rfloor$ is the greatest integer less than or equal to x. For example, $\lfloor 2.5 \rfloor = 2$ and $\lfloor -2.5 \rfloor = -3$.

20. Compute the third digit from the left of 11^{11}.

21. In triangle ABC with $AB = 8$, point D is on side BC such that $BD = DC = AD = 5$. Compute AC.

22. How many permutations (rearrangements) of $(1, 2, 3, 4, 5, 6)$ have at least one **odd** fixed point (number such that the number is in the same point in which it started)? For example, the permutation $(3, 2, 1, 6, 5, 4)$ has exactly two fixed points (which are 2 and 5) and one odd fixed point (which is 5).

23. In equiangular hexagon $ABCDEF$, $AB = 2, CD = 4, DE = 6$, and $EF = 6$. What is the area of $ABCDEF$? Express your answer in simplest radical form.

24. In a future society, there are 25 hours in a day, so 25-hour digital clocks go from 0:00 to 24:59. How many times in one 25-hour day does one of these digital clocks show a palindrome? (Note that times between 1:00 and 9:59 are written without a leading 0, and times between 0:00 and 0:59 are written with three digits. For example, 2:56 would not be written as 02:56, and 0:19 would not be written as 00:19 or :19.)

25. On a desolate road, there is a $\frac{1}{2}$ chance of a car appearing in any 20 minute interval. If the probability of a car appearing at any given time is uniform, what is the probability that in a 90 minute period, no cars will appear? Express your answer as a common fraction in simplest radical form.

26. The number 1600040001 is the product of four distinct primes. What is the sum of these four primes?

27. An infinite plane is tiled with hexagons of side length 2. If a coin of radius 1 is thrown such that it lands on any point in the plane with uniform probability, what is the

probability that it is completely inside a hexagon? Express your answer as a common fraction in simplest radical form.

28. What is the sum of the real solutions to $x^4 + 4x^3 + 5x^2 + 4x + 1 = 0$?

29. Squares $DEBA$, $FGCB$, and $HIAC$ are constructed outwardly from the three sides of triangle ABC. If $AB = AC = 10$ and $BC = 12$, compute the area of hexagon $DEFGHI$.

30. Alex writes down an integer N on a blackboard. Next, if the number on the board is even, she divides it by 2 and writes down the result. If the number on the board is odd, she instead subtracts 1 from it, multiplies it by 3, and writes down the result. Then she erases the old number. She then repeats this process starting with the new number she has written down. After repeating for a while, she has the number 0 on the board. If her original number N was positive and less than 1000, how many different numbers could she have started with?

Name: _____

Grade: _____

School: _____

place ID sticker inside this box	Score: #1 _____ Scorer's Initials _____ Score: #2 _____ Scorer's Initials _____

1. Assume 0.9 Roman miles = 1 standard mile. The Soothsayer wants to warn Julius Caesar to "beware the Ides of March!" but Caesar is 2.025 Roman miles away. The Soothsayer can run 5 standard miles per hour. How many minutes will it take him to get to Caesar to issue his ominous prophecy? Round your answer to the nearest minute.

1.

2. How many positive square divisors does 10000 have?

2.

Name: _____

Grade: _____

School: _____

place ID sticker inside this box

Score: #3 _____ Scorer's Initials _____

Score: #4 _____ Scorer's Initials _____

3. Jimmy's son is one-fourth of Jimmy's age, but five years ago Jimmy was 9 times as old as his son. How old is Jimmy's son?

3.

4. The lines $y = mx + b$ and $y = bx + m$ intersect at $(12, 26)$. Compute the value of $m + b$.

4.

Name: _____

Grade: _____

School: _____

place ID sticker inside this box

Score: #5 _____ Scorer's Initials _____

Score: #6 _____ Scorer's Initials _____

5. The prestigious Manthasy Trophy is awarded to writers who incorporate fantasy into their math problems. From a pool of 6000 writers, only one-thirtieth of $\frac{1}{2}$ of 0.1% receive the award annually on average. How many authors receive the trophy each year on average? Express your answer as a decimal.

5.

6. A parallelogram has vertices $(13, 7)$, $(4, 5)$, $(10, 13)$, and (x, y). What is the sum of all possible values of x?

6.

Name: _____

Grade: _____

School: _____

place ID sticker inside this box

Score: #7 _____ Scorer's Initials _____

Score: #8 _____ Scorer's Initials _____

7. In a country, license plates consist of 4 digits and 2 letters. If the digits and letters can be ordered any way, how many possible license plates are there?

7.

8. A sequence A_n satisfies $A_n = \frac{A_{n-1} - (2n-1)2^{n-1}}{n}$ for $n > 1$, and $A_1 = 2016! - 2$. If $A_{2014} = x \cdot 2^{100} + y$, where x and y are integers, and $0 \leq y < 2^{100}$, compute y.

8.

Team Test
Round 11516

School/
Team:

Score: #1 _____ Scorer's Initials _____

Score: #2 _____ Scorer's Initials _____

name or ID sticker goes in this box

name or ID sticker goes in this box

name or ID sticker goes in this box

name or ID sticker goes in this box

name or ID sticker goes in this box

name or ID sticker goes in this box

1.

2.

3.

4.

5.

6.

7.

8.

9.

10.

Team Test - Round 11516 - © 2015 mathleague.org

1. A cube is composed of 27 smaller cubes, each of volume 1 cubic cubit. The center cube and the 6 cubes at the centers of each face are removed Jenga style. What is the surface area of what remains of the cube, in square cubits?

2. Jack has a 4-digit street address. If the digits sum to 31, how many different addresses could he have?

3. Compute the remainder when the sum of the first 2015 positive integers is divided by 1000.

4. Gary has up to 200 square feet of land with which he must create a rectangular plot with integer dimensions. He has exactly 64 feet of fencing to bound his land. If he must use all of the fencing and can only create one rectangular plot of land, what is the lowest possible percentage of land that he must waste?

5. Two leprechauns decide to celebrate "the Pi Day of the Century" and St. Patrick's day by creating a crop circle with a giant shamrock inside. Emerging from their post-party haze, though, they discover they have actually produced three differently-sized circles, each of which is tangent to the other two. Let A, B, and C be the circles, and let a, b, and c be the radii of those circles, respectively. If $a + b = 5$ hectometers, $a = b - 1$ hectometers, and $b = \frac{c}{a}$, what is the total area of the three circles, in square hectometers?

6. Let $ABCD$ be a square of side length 24. Let M be the midpoint of $\overline{AD}$, and let N be the point on $\overline{CD}$ such that $CN = 6$. Define X to be the point on $\overline{AB}$ such that $\overline{AN}$ is perpendicular to $\overline{MX}$. Compute the length of AX.

7. Compute the sum of all positive integers which have the property that the sum of the digits of the number plus the number itself equal 2014.

8. Five boys and five girls are playing a dodgeball game. There are two teams, team S and team B. Team S will have six people and team B will have four people. Compute the probability that all of the girls are on team S. Express your answer as a common fraction.

9. If a and b are real numbers such that $16 + (a^2 + 1)(b^2 + 1) = 8a + 8b$, compute $a^2 + b^2$.

10. A rabbit is on a number line starting at 1. Every minute, the rabbit hops one unit to the left or right with equal probability. However, if the rabbit ever jumps left from 1 to 0, it is immediately sent back to 1. What is the average number of minutes it will take for the rabbit to reach 4?

1. 28 increased by three times a number is 82. What is the number?

2. Compute $16^2 + 16 + 1$.

3. Calculate: 31^2.

4. If $\frac{1}{x} + 2y = 4$ and $y = \frac{3}{2}$, compute x.

5. Simplify: $\left(\frac{125}{729}\right)^{-1/3}$. Express your answer as a common fraction.

6. I am choosing a team out of 7 people. In how many ways can I choose a team with at least 4 members?

7. Four fair six-sided dice are rolled. What is the probability that the sum of those four numbers is odd? Express your answer as a common fraction.

8. An equilateral triangle is constructed on the side of a square with side length 6. If the combined area of the square and the triangle can be expressed as $a + b\sqrt{c}$, compute $a + b + c$.

9. The angles of a pentagon have degree measures that are consecutive even integers. What is the number of degrees in the measure of the smallest angle?

10. A coin is flipped 5 times. What is the probability of getting at least 4 of the same flips (for example, 4 heads and 1 tail, or all 5 tails)?

11. What is the sum of all the even integers between 0 and 120, inclusive?

12. Billy, Dan, and Jenny are in a line. Billy can't stand next to Dan. Who's in the middle of their line?

13. What is the minimum sum of three positive integers whose product is 342?

14. The Hulk's vertical jump increases by 50% every jump. If his first jump is 64 feet high, how many feet high does he jump on his first jump higher than 500 feet?

15. How many values of x satisfy $(1234 + x)^2 = x^2$?

16. What is $1^1 + 2^2 + 3^3 + 4^4$?

17. Compute: $\binom{9}{0} + \binom{9}{1} + \binom{9}{2} + \binom{9}{3} + \binom{9}{4}$.

18. A plane passes through the center of a sphere, and it intersects with the sphere to form a circle. The sphere's radius is increased so that the area of the circle increases

by 125%. What is the ratio of the new volume to the original volume of the sphere? Express your answer as a common fraction.

19. A quadrilateral has integer side lengths. Three of its sides have lengths of 4, 8, and 9. What is the positive difference between the maximum and minimum length of the fourth side?

20. Compute the ratio of the number of permutations of the 10-letter string $ABBBBBBBBB$ to the number of permutations of the 10-letter string $AABBBBBBBB$.

21. What is the slope of the line passing through the points $(7, 3)$ and $(-8, 20)$? Express your answer as a common fraction.

22. Compute the surface area of a regular tetrahedron with side length 4.

23. Two roots of the equation $3x^3 - 12x^2 + px + q = 0$ are 8 and 3. Find the third root of the equation.

24. I read 4 pages every 7 minutes. In 7 hours, how many 30-page books can I read?

25. What is the cube root of $15^2 - 3^2$?

26. John rolls a pair of six-sided dice twice; each time, he adds the numbers showing. What is the probability that at least one of the two sums is 7?

27. If the volume of a sphere is numerically equal to three times the surface area of the sphere, what is the radius of the sphere?

28. Aaron and Erin are flipping a coin. Aaron wins when the sequence HHH first shows up, and Erin wins when the sequence THH shows up (where H and T represent heads and tails respectively). They keep flipping the coin until someone wins. What is the probability that Erin wins? Express your answer as a common fraction.

29. How many natural numbers less than 2000 do not contain the digit 6?

30. Compute the average of the mean, median, and mode of the set $\{0, 1, 2, 2, 3, 3, 3\}$. Express your answer as a common fraction.

31. Ryan bought a jersey originally priced at $86 for $55.90. What is the percent discount given by the store?

32. For collinear points A, B, and C, B is in between A and C. $A = (2, -1)$, $B = (8, 2)$ and $AB = 3BC$. Compute the sum of the coordinates of point C.

33. The four numbers a, b, c, and d satisfy the relations $\frac{a}{b} = 9$, $\frac{b}{c} = \frac{2}{3}$, and $\frac{c}{d} = 16$. What is $\frac{a}{d}$?

34. Find the sum of all integers n such that $n^2 < 100n$.

35. How many 2-digit integers contain a 4 as one of their digits?

36. Compute the area of a trapezoid with bases 16 and 84 and height 152.

37. A quadrilateral has its vertices chosen from a 6 by 6 grid of points one unit apart. What is the area of the largest possible quadrilateral that satisfies this condition?

38. As a decimal, $\frac{1}{27}$ can be written as $0.xyzxyzxyz\ldots$ where x, y, z are digits. Compute the product xyz.

39. If 2 sides of a right triangle have length 7 and 13, what is the least possible value of the third side? Express your answer in simplest radical form.

40. What is the remainder when 6! is divided by 7?

41. On a map, two cities are 21 centimeters apart. The map legend indicates that 1 centimeter = 2.5 kilometers. How many meters apart are the actual cities?

42. Evaluate the product $P = \left(1 - \frac{1}{2}\right)\left(1 - \frac{1}{3}\right)\cdots\left(1 - \frac{1}{2015}\right)$. Express your answer as a common fraction.

43. A biologist catches 63 bass from a lake, tags them, and then releases them back into the lake. The next day, the biologist comes back and catches 72 bass and finds out that 18 of them have tags. Based on this data, what is the best integer estimate for the number of bass that live in that lake?

44. If $x = (y - 2)^2$ and $y = (x - 4)^2$ and $x - y = 4$, compute $x + y$.

45. How many ways are there to arrange 10 books in a row if 4 of them are indistinguishable?

46. Compute the sum of the two smallest prime numbers less than 100.

47. Six people decide to have a book sharing party and each of them brings one book. The books are shuffled and randomly passed back, one to each person, such that no one receives their own book. In how many ways can this happen?

48. The gravitational force exerted by two objects on each other is inversely proportional to the square of the distance between the objects. Two rocks are initially $9\sqrt{3}$ meters

apart. If the distance between them is changed such that the gravitational force they exert on each other is tripled, how far, in meters, are they now separated by?

49. What is the 100th term in the arithmetic sequence -3, 5, 13, 21...?

50. Compute the sum of the squares of the digits of $\sqrt{9^2 + 12^2 + 36^2}$.

51. Evaluate: 44×44.

52. Compute $\frac{3+6+9+12}{7+14+21+28}$ as a common fraction.

53. The arithmetic mean of 22 numbers is 304. What is their sum?

54. An equal number of pennies, dimes, and quarters were used to convert $18 to coins. How many coins, in total, were used?

55. How many positive five-digit integers contain no digit greater than 4?

56. What is 12% of 25 added to 25% of 12?

57. What is the greatest perfect square less than 5000?

58. What is the largest odd divisor of 8! ?

59. Sandy has 15 dollars to spend on notebooks, which cost 1 dollar, and binders, which cost 4 dollars. How many combinations of notebooks and binders can Sandy buy, if she must spend all of her money?

60. The digits 1, 2, 3, 4 are permuted to make a 4-digit number. What is the probability that this number is divisible by 4? Express your answer as a common fraction.

61. If the lengths of the major axes of an ellipse are 5 and 9, what is the area of the ellipse? Express your answer in terms of π.

62. How many digits does 200^{10} have?

63. A certain species of bacteria doubles in population every 3 hours. If a container starts off with one bacterium, how many whole days would it take for the total number of bacteria to exceed 2 million?

64. James can shovel 24 driveways in 16 hours. How many hours will it take him to shovel 54 driveways?

65. How many multiples of 3 are greater than 200 but less than 600?

66. A square has area 81. What is its perimeter?

67. At a speed of 45 miles per hour, how many hours would it take to travel 720 miles?

68. How many different ways are there to arrange the letters in the word GREET?

69. Find the mode of the following set: 6, 7, 4, 8, 3, 3, 6, 4, 4, 7, 8, 9.

70. A class of 12 students is choosing a president and vice-president. How many ways are there to do this?

71. Evaluate: 63×15.

72. Compute the sum of the digits of 101^5.

73. If one angle of a rhombus is 30 degrees and one side has a length of 12, what is the area of the rhombus? Express your answer in simplest radical form.

74. In triangle ABC, $AB = BC = 4$ and $\angle B = 120°$. Compute AC.

75. If a prism has a length, width, and height of a, $6a$, and $5a$, and its volume is at most 2015, what is the largest possible integer value of a?

76. Find the smallest palindrome greater than 1000 that is not divisible by 11.

77. Three positive integers have a sum of 25. What is the maximum possible product of those numbers?

78. Find the units digit of 6^{2015}.

79. The top three winners in a math competition share the prize money in the ratio 9:5:2. If they win a total of $6752, how many dollars does the top prize winner receive?

80. If $x^2 = 8x + 9$ and x is negative, find x.

Sprint Test

1. 17
2. 29
3. 21
4. 350
5. 15
6. 2112
7. 18
8. 11
9. 3
10. 53
11. 216 (milliliters)
12. 8191
13. $\frac{625}{1296}$
14. 1165
15. 22
16. 98
17. 12
18. 5
19. 0.25
20. 5
21. 6
22. 294
23. $50\sqrt{3}$
24. 71
25. $\frac{\sqrt{2}}{32}$
26. 19020
27. $\frac{4-2\sqrt{3}}{3}$
28. -3
29. 536
30. 10

Target Test

1. 27 (minutes)
2. 9
3. 8
4. 4
5. 0.1
6. 27
7. 101400000
8. 4062240

Team Test

1. 72 (square cubits)
2. 56
3. 120
4. 4 (%)
5. 49π (square hm)
6. 16
7. 3994
8. $\frac{1}{42}$
9. 14
10. 12 (minutes)

Countdown

1. 18
2. 273
3. 961
4. 1
5. $\frac{9}{5}$
6. 64
7. $\frac{1}{2}$
8. 48
9. 104
10. $\frac{3}{8}$
11. 3540
12. Jenny
13. 28
14. 729 (feet)
15. 1
16. 288
17. 256
18. $\frac{27}{8}$
19. 19
20. $\frac{2}{9}$.
21. $-\frac{17}{15}$
22. $16\sqrt{3}$
23. -7
24. 8
25. 6
26. $\frac{11}{36}$

27. 9
28. $\frac{7}{8}$
29. 1457
30. $\frac{7}{3}$
31. 35 (%)
32. 13
33. 96
34. 4950
35. 18
36. 7600
37. 25
38. 0
39. $2\sqrt{30}$
40. 6
41. 52500
42. $\frac{1}{2015}$
43. 252
44. 4
45. 151200
46. 5
47. 265
48. 9
49. 789
50. 90
51. 1936
52. $\frac{3}{7}$
53. 6688

54. 150
55. 2500
56. 6
57. 4900
58. 315
59. 4
60. $\frac{1}{4}$
61. $\frac{45\pi}{4}$
62. 24
63. 3
64. 36
65. 133
66. 36
67. 16
68. 60
69. 4
70. 132
71. 945
72. 14
73. 72
74. $4\sqrt{3}$
75. 4
76. 10001
77. 576
78. 6
79. 3798
80. -1

Sprint Test Solutions

1. The standard chessboard has $8^2 = 64$ squares, and the expanded one has $9^2 = 81$, so the number that must be added is $81 - 64 = 17$.

2. List them all: 2, 3, 5, 7, 11, 13, 17, 19, 23, 29, 31, 37, 41, 43, 47, 53, 59, 61, 67, 71, 73, 79, 83, 89, 97, 101, 103, 107, 109. The answer is 29.

3. The quickest way is to note that $8000 = 20^3$, and so the product will be slightly too small if the middle number is 20. 21 clearly works.

4. $216+125+64+27+8+1-36-25-16-9-4-1 = 350$

5. Each sister got one-half of one-third of one-half, or one-twelfth of the 180 candies.

6. Together they can compliment 22 per hour or 176 per day. Over 12 days, the total is 2112. Their stamina is impressive; it is hard to endure Klingon opera, much less invent nice things to say about it.

7. If the circle has area 9π, its radius is 3. This means each side of the square has length $3\sqrt{2}$ and the area is 18.

8. Since $2^{10} = 1024$, it will bounce $\frac{1}{1024}$ as high 10 bounces after the first which is just under 1 meter.

9. Keeping track of areas, widths, and lengths is not necessary. We just multiply the two one-dimensional ratios to get the two-dimensional ratios in each case. So Saurav is $\frac{3}{2}$ of the area of Chewbacca while Chandan is 3 Chewbaccas in area. Chandan is twice as large as Saurav, so Chandan is the largest and Chewbacca is the smallest.

10. $901 = 53 \cdot 17$, and $2014 = 53 \cdot 38$. Since 17 and 38 are relatively prime, the GCD is 53.

11. Each of the 6 sides has an area of 10000 square centimeters, and an 80cm by 80cm unpainted square in the center, leaving a total of 3600 square centimeters painted on each of 6 sides

for a total of 21600 square centimeters, or 2.16 square meters to paint.

12. Let x be the desired sum. Notice that $x + 1 = 2^0 + 2^0 + 2^1 + ... + 2^{12} = 2^1 + 2^1 + 2^2 + ... + 2^{12} = 2^2 + 2^2 + ... = ... = 2^{12} + 2^{12} = 2^{13}$. Thus $x = 2^{13} - 1 = 8191$.

13. The probability of not drawing a red toy is $\frac{5}{6}$. Take this to the 4th power to get $\frac{625}{1296}$.

14. 121021_3 is $(1 \cdot 3^5) + (2 \cdot 3^4) + (1 \cdot 3^3) + 0 + (2 \cdot 3^1) + (1 \cdot 3^0) = 439_{10}$. Since $439 = 343 + 49 + 42 + 5$, this is 1165 in base 7.

15. If he has a 10, he can only have 0,1,3, or 5 1s, the others being determined for 4 ways. There is only one way with 3 5s. With 2 5s, we can have 0, 1, or 2 2s. With 1 5 and no 10, the number of 2s can be 0,1,2,3,4, or 5, and with no 5s or 10s, we can have 0,1,2,3,4,5,6, or 7 2s for a total of 22 ways.

16. Since $13035 = 3 \cdot 5 \cdot 11 \cdot 79$, the sum of the prime factors is $3 + 5 + 11 + 79 = 98$.

17. There is only one way to get to each of steps 2, 3, and 4. After this, the number of ways to get to a step is just the sum of the number of ways to get to the steps 2 and 3 below it. So the number of ways to get to steps 5 through 12 are, respectively, 2,2,3,4,5,7,9, and 12.

18. Using the first two relations, we can replace an eagle with an aardvark and a springbok to see that two aardvarks and a springbok equal a duck, and so four aardvarks and two springboks equal two ducks which equal three springboks by the third relation. So a springbok weighs the same as four aardvarks. From the second relation, we see now that an eagle equals five aardvarks.

19. If x is in between 0 and 1, then $\lfloor x \rfloor = 0$. Then, $x = \frac{1}{k}$ for some integer k. If $k > 8$, then the left-hand side is 1 but the right-hand side is less than 1. If $6 \le k \le 8$, the left-hand side is $\frac{1}{2}$, but the right-hand side is less than $\frac{1}{2}$. If $k = 5$, then the left-hand side is 3, but the right-hand

side is $\frac{1}{5}$. When $k = 4$, both sides are $\frac{1}{4}$, so the smallest possible positive x is $\frac{1}{4} = 0.25$.

20. Note that $11^n = (10+1)^n = 10^n + n \cdot 10^{n-1} + \binom{n}{2} \cdot 10^{n-2} + \dots$. For $n = 11$, none of the binomial coefficients $\binom{11}{k}$ is larger than 1000, so the third decimal digit is only directly affected by the first 5 terms of this expansion. However, the fourth decimal digit is affected by the 6th term of this expansion, and may carry over to the third digit. The sum of the first 6 terms is $10^{11} + 11 \cdot 10^{10} + 55 \cdot 10^9 + 165 \cdot 10^8 + 330 \cdot 10^7 + 462 \cdot 10^6$. This is equal to $10^6 \cdot (100000 + 110000 + 55000 + 16500 + 3300 + 462) = 10^6 \cdot 285262$. Note that the fifth decimal digit cannot possibly carry over to the fourth digit enough to make it carry over to the third digit again, so the third digit is 5.

21. Note that D is the circumcenter of ABC, so $\overline{BC}$ is a diameter of the circumcircle, and thus $\angle BAC = 90°$. Then $AC = \sqrt{10^2 - 8^2} = 6$.

22. Let A be the set of all permutations that include 1 as a fixed point, and similarly define B and C for 3 and 5. Then, by PIE, we want $|A \cup B \cup C| = |A| + |B| + |C| - |A \cap B| - |B \cap C| - |C \cap A| + |A \cap B \cap C|$. Note that $|A| = |B| = |C| = 5!$, $|A \cap B| = |B \cap C| = |C \cap A| = 4!$, and $|A \cap B \cap C| = 3!$. So our answer is $3(120) - 3(24) + 6 = 294$.

23. Extend sides BC, DE, and FA. Call the intersection of BC and FA point X, the intersection of FA and DE point Y, and the intersection of BC and DE point Z. Note that XYZ is equilateral, since each of its angles is 60 degrees. Also, triangles AXB, CYD, and EZF are equilateral. It is easy to see then that the side length of XYZ is $4+6+6 = 16$, so it has an area of $64\sqrt{3}$. The areas of AXB, CYD, and EZF are $\sqrt{3}$, $4\sqrt{3}$ and $9\sqrt{3}$ respectively, so the area of $ABCDEF$ is $64\sqrt{3} - (9+4+1)\sqrt{3} = 50\sqrt{3}$.

24. If the hour is before 10, then the time has 3 digits. The last digit can always be the same as the first one, and there are 6 possibilities for the middle digit, so the total number of palindromes is $6 \cdot 10 = 60$. If the hour is 10 or after, then the time has 4 digits. If the first and last digits are both 1, then there are 6 possibilities for the middle digits. If the first and last digits are both 2, then there are 5 possibilites for the middle digits, because 25:52 is not a valid time. This is a total of 71.

25. Let x be the probability that no car appears in a 10 minute interval. The probability that no car appears in a 20 minute interval is $1 - \frac{1}{2} = \frac{1}{2}$, and a 20 minute interval is two 10 minute intervals in a row, so $x^2 = \frac{1}{2} \Rightarrow x = \frac{\sqrt{2}}{2}$. Then, the probability that no car appears in a 90 minute interval is $x^9 = \frac{\sqrt{2}}{32}$.

26. If $x = 200$, we have $1600040001 = x^4 + x^2 + 1 = (x^2 - x + 1) \cdot (x^2 + x + 1)$. This is $39801 \cdot 40201 = 3 \cdot 13267 \cdot 7 \cdot 5743$, so our answer is 19020. (Note that 13267 and 5743 are prime, but it is not necessary to verify this directly, since the problem tells you that the original number is the product of four primes.)

27. Consider the center of the coin, O, and the hexagon it lands in. Note that the center has an equal probability of landing in any point in any hexagon. For the coin to be completely inside the hexagon, the center must be at least a distance of 1 from each edge of the hexagon. Suppose it lands in hexagon ABCDEF. Then, the span of the hexagon (the distance between AB and DE) is $2\sqrt{3}$. For the center to be at least a distance of 1 from each edge of the hexagon, it must be in a similar hexagon centered at the center of ABCDEF and oriented the same way, with a span of $2\sqrt{3} - 2$. This means the distance between any point on the boundary of the smaller hexagon and ABCDEF is at least 1, and any point outside the smaller hexagon and inside ABCDEF will be a distance less than 1 away from some side of ABCDEF. Then, the probability of the center of the coin landing in the smaller hexagon is the ratio of the areas of the hexagons, which is $\frac{(2\sqrt{3}-2)^2}{(2\sqrt{3})^2} = \frac{4-2\sqrt{3}}{3}$.

28. Note that $x^4 + 4x^3 + 5x^2 + 4x + 1 = (x^4 + 4x^3 + 6x^2 + 4x + 1) - x^2 = (x^2 + 2x + 1)^2 - x^2 = (x^2 + 3x + 1)(x^2 + x + 1)$. $x^2 + x + 1 = 0$ does not have real roots, but $x^2 + 3x + 1 = 0$ does, and their sum is -3.

29. The area of triangle ABC is $\frac{12 \cdot 8}{2} = 48$. The area of the three squares are 100, 100, and 144. It remains to find the areas of the three outer triangles that each have two side lengths of squares. First consider triangle DAI, which has the properties $AD = AB$, $AI = AC$, and $\angle DAI = 180 - \angle DAI$. Thus, we have $[DAI] = \frac{1}{2} \cdot AB \cdot AC \cdot \sin(180 - \angle BAC) = \frac{1}{2} \cdot AB \cdot AC \cdot \sin \angle BAC$. But notice that this is exactly the area of triangle ABC if we were to use the sine area formula with included angle $\angle BAC$, so $[DAI] = [ABC]$. The same

Target Test Solutions

1. 2.025 Roman miles is equivalent to $\frac{2.025}{0.9} = 2.25$ standard miles. If the Soothsayer can run 5 standard miles per hour, it will take him $\frac{2.25}{5} = .45$ hours to travel the distance. Since $(0.45)(60) = 27$ minutes, that is how long it will take the Soothsayer to reach Caesar. Sadly, despite the Soothsayer's efforts, which include him trying to maintain a steady speed while running up and down several of the hills of Rome, his warning is fated to be ignored. Perhaps a good technical writing course would help him to issue more specific prophesies.

2. $10000 = 2^4 \cdot 5^4$. Any number which is a square factor must have all even exponents in its prime factorization, so the exponents that work for both 2 and 5 are 0, 2, and 4. With 3 possibilities for each prime factor, there are 9 such factors.

3. Let Jimmy's age be a. Then his son's age is $\frac{1}{4}a$, so $a - 5 = 9(\frac{1}{4}a - 5)$. Then $a = 32$, so his son's age is 8.

4. Both the lines go through the point $(26, 12)$, so $26 = 12m + b$ and $26 = 12b + m$. Then adding

goes for the other triangles, so our answer is $4 \cdot 48 + 100 + 100 + 144 = 536$.

30. The only way Alex can ever write down 0 is if her second-to-last number is 1, so we want to know how many different starting numbers will lead her to 1. Notice that if at any time, the number she has is divisible by 3, then the next number she writes down will also be divisible by 3. Thus if she is ever going to reach 1, she cannot write down any other odd number–because if she does, then all the numbers she ever writes down after that will be divisible by 3, which prevents her from reaching 1. If all she writes down are even numbers, then she will keep dividing them by 2 until she reaches 1, which means she must start with a power of 2. There are 10 powers of 2 less than 1000.

gives $52 = 13(m + b)$ so $m + b = 4$.

5. $(6000)(\frac{1}{30})(0.5)(0.001) = 0.1$ Thus only one-tenth of an author receives the award annually. Conversely, we could say that one writer wins the award every ten years; this rarity is why the Inscribed Unicorn is such a prestigious trophy.

6. Note that reflecting any given vertex over the midpoint of the other line segment formed by the other two vertices gives a valid point (x, y) for the fourth vertex of the parallelogram, and it is easy to see that only these three points work. Then, the possible fourth points have x-values $13 + 4 - 10$, $13 + 10 - 4$, and $-13 + 4 + 10$, so the total sum is $13 + 4 + 10 = 27$.

7. There are $\binom{6}{2} = 15$ ways to choose the ways to order the letters and digits, and $26^2 \cdot 10^4$ ways to choose the letters and digits, so the total number is $15 \cdot 26^2 \cdot 10^4 = 101400000$.

8. Note that $n(A_n + 2^n) = A_{n-1} + 2^{n-1}$. Then, $n!(A_n + 2^n) = (n-1)!(A_{n-1} + 2^{n-1})$, so $k!(A_k + 2^k)$ is the same for all values of k. Thus $1!(A_1 + 2^1) = 2016! = 2014!(A_{2014} + 2^{2014})$, so $A_{2014} = 2016 \cdot 2015 - 2^{2014}$, so $x = -2^{1914}$ and $y = 2016 \cdot 2015 = 4062240$.

Team Test Solutions

1. The cube starts with a surface area of 54. After removing the single smaller cube in the center, removing each of the central cubes of the faces causes one small face to disappear while exposing a face of its 4 neighbors for a net of 3 more square cubits each. $54 + 18 = 72$.

2. We will list the possible sets of digits with the number of permutations of each in parentheses. 9994(4), 9985(12), 9976(12), 8886(12), 9877(12), and 8887(4) for a total of 56.

3. The sum is equal to $2015 \cdot 1008$, and the last 3 digits of this are $8 \cdot 15 = 120$.

4. Letting the length and width respectively of the plot be a and b, we want ab to be as close to 200 as possible while being below 200, given that $a + b = 32$. We can check a few numbers: $20 \cdot 12 = 240$, too big; $22 \cdot 10 = 220$, still too big; $23 \cdot 9 = 207$, still too big, but $24 \cdot 8 = 192$, which is the largest product smaller than 200. Therefore, Gary wastes 8 square feet of land, or $8/200 = 4\%$.

5. Using substitution, we see that $(b - 1) + b = 5$ hectometers, so $b = 3$ hectometers. Then $a = 3 - 1 = 2$ hectometers. If $b = \frac{c}{a}$, then $c = ab = 6$ hectometers. The area of A is thus 4π hectometers^2, B is 9π hectometers^2, and C is 36π hectometers^2. $36 + 9 + 4 = 49$ so the total area of the strange non-shamrock circles is 49πhm^2. The leprechauns are disappointed at the shape, but the consternation of the local farmer, who finds his field of spring cabbages destroyed, is all the two pranksters could wish for.

6. We have $\angle AXM = \angle DAN = 90° - \angle NAX$,

so $\triangle DAN$ and $\triangle AXM$ are similar. Since $\frac{AX}{AM} = \frac{AD}{DN}$, $AX = 12 \cdot \frac{24}{18} = 16$.

7. Let $s(n)$ denote the sum of the digits of n. Note that n has to be pretty close to 2014, since $s(n)$ is small compared to n. In particular, if $n \le 2014$, then $s(n) \le 2 + 9 + 9 + 9 = 29$, so $n \ge 2014 - 29 = 1985$. For $1985 \le n \le 1989$, we want $1 + 9 + 8 + d + 1980 + d = 2014$, so $d = 8$ and $n = 1988$. There are no integer solutions to the corresponding equation for $1990 \le n \le 1999$. For $2000 \le n \le 2009$ we have a solution at 2006, and there are no remaining solutions, so our answer is $1988 + 2006 = 3994$.

8. There are $\binom{10}{6} = 210$ ways to determine team S. If all the girls are on team S, there are $\binom{5}{1} = 5$ ways to determine the last boy, so our answer is $\frac{5}{210} = \frac{1}{42}$.

9. To exploit the symmetry this equation suggests, let $x = a + b$ and $y = ab$. Then $a^2 + b^2 = x^2 - 2y$, so the equation becomes $16 + y^2 + x^2 - 2y + 1 = 8x$. Rearranging this gives $(y - 1)^2 + (x - 4)^2 = 0$, so $y = 1$ and $x = 4$, and thus $a^2 + b^2 = 14$.

10. Let a be the expected number of steps it takes the rabbit to get from 1 to 2, and let b and c similarly be the expected number of steps it takes the rabbit to get from 2 to 3 and 3 to 4, respectively. At 1, there is an equal chance the rabbit will move to 2 immediately or stay at 1, so $a = \frac{1}{2} + \frac{1}{2}(1 + a) = 1 + \frac{1}{2}a$, from which $a = 2$. At 2, it has an equal chance of moving to 3 or 1, so $b = \frac{1}{2} + \frac{1}{2}(1 + a + b) = 2 + \frac{1}{2}b$, so $b = 4$. Finally, at 3, it has an equal chance of moving to 4 or 3, so $c = \frac{1}{2} + \frac{1}{2}(1 + b + c) = 3 + \frac{1}{2}c$, so $c = 6$, and $a + b + c = 12$.